T0243402

STRATEGIES FOR
ORGANIZATION
DESIGN

TIFFANY McDOWELL, PhD

STRATEGIES FOR
ORGANIZATION
DESIGN

USING THE PEOPLETECTURE MODEL

TO IMPROVE COLLABORATION

AND PERFORMANCE

WILEY

Published by John Wiley & Sons, Inc., Hoboken, New Jersey.
Published simultaneously in Canada.

For general information on our other products and services or for technical support, please contact our Customer Care Department within the United States at (800) 762-2974, outside the United States at (317) 572-3993 or fax (317) 572-4002.

Wiley also publishes its books in a variety of electronic formats. Some content that appears in print may not be available in electronic formats. For more information about Wiley products, visit our web site at www.wiley.com.

Library of Congress Cataloging-in-Publication Data is Available:

ISBN 9781394170968 (Hardback)
ISBN 9781394170975 (ePub)
ISBN 9781394170982 (ePDF)

Cover Design and Image: Wiley

SKY10041166_011223

This book is dedicated to my father, Mickey McDowell, PhD

Contents

Preface   *ix*

Chapter 1 Right Intentions, Wrong Focus   1

Chapter 2 Solving the Right Problem   9

Chapter 3 The Peopletecture Model   19

Chapter 4 Hierarchy   25

Chapter 5 Networks   37

Chapter 6 Hierarchy Versus Networks   59

Chapter 7 Measurement   65

Chapter 8 Membership   83

Chapter 9 Responsibility   97

Chapter 10 Teaming   111

Chapter 11 Purpose and Utility   121

Chapter 12 Peopletecture for Individuals and Managers   139

Chapter 13 Where Should You Start?   149

Chapter 14 Conclusion: What's Next?   157

Appendix   169

References   179

Bibliography   193

About the Author   205

Acknowledgments   207

Index   209

Preface

What is perhaps my greatest professional achievement—helping one of the world's top CEOs design his organization to adapt, thrive and post impressive earnings—started under strained circumstances.

My team faced high stakes and expectations from the start. It was 18 months after the largest acquisition in the company's 70-year history, and despite each company's success before the acquisition, the combined entity was not living up to its promise. The CEO was under enormous pressure to improve share price and deliver on the combined company's value to shareholders. That's where we came in.

We began by simply trying to get the executives from the two legacy organizations to work better together. This included workshops to air out differences and practice "enterprise mindset" thinking and behaviors. Unfortunately, not much changed.

We held another workshop to focus on a shared decision model, establishing an executive charter that encouraged "horizontal teaming." It also included an interactive session on implicit bias we all have as humans when we make decisions. Everyone reported they enjoyed the experience, but it didn't seem like we had moved the needle much, and share price remained flat.

The frustrated CEO hired an executive coach for each of his direct reports in an attempt to change their individual behavior and get them to start acting like a team. But my colleague and I felt it was time to propose a more systemic intervention—one that we really believed would help the CEO finally put an end to the territory grabs, internal competition, gaming the system, and political turf wars, to name just a few of the ineffective behaviors we were seeing (and that we see in many large organizations).

We gathered data to aid our pitch to the CEO. We took some existing information on their corporate relationships and analyzed it at length to come up with a different approach—something we had not done before at this scale. We were both excited and nervous as our next CEO meeting loomed.

The day arrived, and we filed into headquarters with purpose. Stepping out of the elevator, I nervously checked my teeth on my phone camera to make sure my lipstick wasn't smudged. I took a deep breath and smiled. With my colleague next to me, we marched with great intentions into our client's office. The CEO looked up from the stack of papers on his desk, peered over his computer at us, and said, "Oh, it's the consultants, come to point out my faults and tell me how to do things better!" Gulp. But then he let out a big laugh and invited us to sit down.

After the requisite small talk, the CEO abruptly turned to the matter at hand, "So, you have done all this analysis on my company, what's the punchline? And please, no death by slides." I subtly placed my 50-page PowerPoint deck in my lap, a deck that was filled with beautiful pictures and data that I had been overly prepared to present. I stared down at my new Louboutins for a moment. I cleared my throat. "Well, let me start with the highlights, and then we can dive into any details you like.

"You have called out several business issues. One is that you acquired quite a few strong leaders onto your executive team that have amazing resumes and track records, yet they are not collaborating effectively with your more tenured executives, nor are any of them making progress against your strategy. Now you are questioning whether you made the wrong talent decisions.

"Another is that you bought into the 'agile' framework and put pods and squads and such things in place to create an empowered network of cross-functional teams, but instead of getting an explosion of innovation and growth, the silo walls between your business units have actually become higher and thicker.

"Finally, you told everyone they were empowered to make decisions, but despite this decree, accountability has all but disappeared, and decisions have slowed down even more than before. Until now, much of these tensions were invisible. But we have taken some network data of your executives and their teams, and we have some valuable insights to share. Allow me to show you just one slide." He nodded. (See Figure P.1.)

"Let's look at the key takeaways from this visual. The different shades are your departments. The circles are all the people in the top three levels of the company. The size of the circle represents the

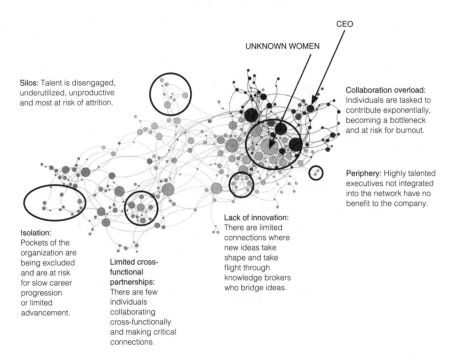

Figure P.1   Network Map of Organization
Source: EY Network Visual

amount of collaboration and influence any one individual might have." He stared at the picture for a while, then he stared at me for an extremely uncomfortable duration—how long is unclear, but it seemed like an eternity. I looked down at my new shoes again. Then I looked back up and went for it.

"I am going to take a chance here and begin with the proverbial elephant in the room. The most influential person in the company is not you. As you can see, the most critical knowledge broker in your whole company is three levels down from you and not connected to you, not focused on your strategy, and totally overloaded with collaboration requirements. She needs to be freed up to be effective."

"What? I've never even heard of that woman!!!"

"Exactly. And furthermore, your key leaders are not aligned to core strategic initiatives because their incentives drive them to work at cross-purposes, and some of your newer execs are on the periphery and at risk of leaving, which would be a devastating blow from a leadership and talent perspective. See here," pointing to my one sanctioned page, "there are major breaks in the teams or 'squads' that must be mended to get the innovation needed for growth.

"Finally, because they are not teaming, no one is empowered to work together effectively. But the amazing thing is, now that we have made the invisible visible, we can ACT!" I was practically yelling now. "We can unleash networks of teams, stop collaboration overload, intentionally architect where your people place their energy and attention, create an environment where people feel a strong sense of belonging, and go fast and innovate at the point of the customer."

I took a breath. I noticed the CEO had gone from peering at me over his computer to looking back down at his pile of papers. Another gulp. *Too much consultant-speak*, I chastised myself silently. Seconds passed, but it seemed longer. Then . . .

"Well, I didn't have very high expectations when you walked in here. So, I am pleased to say I am intrigued enough to learn more."

We marched back out of the room with even bigger smiles than before. Actually, I think I was beaming. Our first big breakthrough in bringing a whole new set of insights and interventions to improve how organizations thrive in this ever-changing world of work.

Almost two years later I was sitting in the same office, and I was able to say, honestly, "You killed it on the quarterly earnings call this morning!" My CEO smiled, thanked me and said, "It doesn't hurt that earnings are up 40%! But it's not just about the strong business performance today. I really feel we are positioned in the best way possible to navigate the uncertain future. Letting go of making all the decisions at the top and using the power of network analysis to drive intentional collaboration has actually worked! We got two new products launched in record time! And the market loves us for it!" he laughed. "Yes, I thought you were crazy when you made me put team incentives in place, but it seems to have worked and not cost me too much.

"The other day someone walked up to me and said they felt empowered and that knowing they could take responsibility for company decisions brought meaning to their work and a sense of belonging to our company. A year ago, this seemed like an idealistic dream whose day would never arrive."

Have you ever felt that your company could do better, be better? That it would be easier to get a new job than to move up or get recognized for your contributions in your current job?

Having had many client experiences like the one I just described, I felt compelled to write this book to help more organizations shift their improvement focus from fixing employees to fixing the system, by using insights into how people behave in groups, and by making the invisible visible through network insights. The ideas I will describe in each chapter collectively come together in the Peopletecture Model to comprehensively solve these challenges for the first time, with practical solutions that can be immediately applied to invoke change. If you want to learn how to accelerate organizational transformation in a data-driven, scientifically supported way, to make work more meaningful for all humans, then this book is for you.

1

Right Intentions, Wrong Focus

"Every problem is a gift—without problems we would not grow."
—Anthony Robbins, *Awaken the Giant Within* (2007)

Too many organizations bring in consultants and coaches and architects and a host of other people to try to "fix" employees' experiences and performances, as my experience with the aforementioned global conglomerate showed, in the all-too-often vain hope that these changes will translate into company-wide improvements in productivity, growth and product quality. After more than 20 years of organization strategies consulting, I believe the same three challenges plague traditional organization design:

1. Design decisions are not linked to behavior.
2. Design solutions are focused primarily on the individual.
3. Design ignores the power of horizontal networks.

Design Decisions Are Not Linked to Behavior

The first fundamental gap in the existing models is that they do not clearly link the big, macro decisions that happen at the system level of

1

an organization to the individual and group behaviors that result. However, due to a set of hardwired evolutionary conditions in human brains, the environment an individual or group is in has a direct and predictable influence on feelings and behavior. By understanding the context that has been designed and combining this with the psychology of how humans think and feel, we can understand individual thoughts and behaviors that are the direct outcomes of these design choices.

Let's say Company A wants to reorganize. It used to be organized by its brands. Each brand had a leader, a product team that designed and improved the brand, a marketing team that advertised the brand, and a sales team that sold the brand to customers. There was a great deal of internal competition between brands. One sales team bragged about selling more of one brand than another sales team did and how big their paychecks were, marketing teams were rewarded by increasing the market share of their respective brands, and the company's executive meetings looked more like warfare than an integrated team of professionals working together.

In an effort to meet ever-changing customer demands and grow the company, Company A decides to organize by the solutions customers care about. Instead of just selling its different brands to the same customers, it is going to sell a whole solution that solves customers' problems. The solution will better meet the needs of Company A's loved and respected customers! It will sell more goods and services people need to more people who need them! It will help the enterprise! Everybody wins!

So what does Company A do? It changes the leaders of the brands and tells them they are now leaders of the solutions. The company updates its marketing materials and asks the marketing and sales teams to collaborate to reach customers in a coordinated fashion with the solutions. It asks the engineers in the product teams to collaborate and share ideas and information about how to improve the solutions.

And what happens? Well, the sales teams pretty much ignore the changes at the top and keep engaging with their customers in the same old way. After all, they are paid to sell a brand. How much of that brand they sell directly impacts their paycheck. They would be worse off personally if they followed the new solution structure.

The marketing people are furious with the salespeople because they are now incentivized by solution market share, but the salespeople are not working with them on this. So instead of collaborating, they put up higher and thicker barricades. They don't know or trust each other. Morale quickly plummets, absences increase, and turnover ensues in large numbers. The engineers like working with each other and sharing new ideas across the different brands, but production and innovation slows to a standstill because it is unclear whom they should work with to get solutions to market, given the behavior of the marketing and sales teams. Each team is responding rationally to its unique and separate context but, in doing so, is suboptimizing the enterprise.

Today we talk about organizations' ecosystems and platforms, strategy and transactions, and the operating models and capabilities needed for future success. In addition to the chief executive officer, we have chief strategy officers, chief transformation officers, and various business unit heads. Then, in a totally separate part of the company, we talk about workforce experience and employer brand, incentives and rewards, and hiring and retaining for the workforce of the future. Often these issues are relegated to the chief human resource officer, the chief diversity officer, or some similar title, like chief impact officer or chief people officer. These conversations occur in separate silos, as if they are completely unrelated to one another, but *they are actually one and the same.*

The choices made on how to set up an executive team, their roles, and their accountability for profits have a direct and predictable impact on how middle managers feel and how frontline workers act. We need to use these insights early and often to create an environment where an understanding of human behavior is at the center of the design.

Design Solutions Are Focused Primarily on the Individual

The second, related challenge is that the interventions suggested to remedy the many trials of traditional organizational design in today's environment are almost solely focused on the individual, with only the occasional attempt to address the group. Consider some of the corporate terms you've heard over the years, such as "enterprise mindset" or "collaborative culture." These are typically offered up with little guidance on how to design the context that drives the desired individual and group behavior in the first place. There is much of the "why" at the system level—think "meaningful work" or "shared purpose"—but little of the "how."

This challenge has plagued me for a long time—all the way back to my graduate school days. In my doctoral dissertation on this topic, "How to Have Fun at Work," I hypothesized that there were fun people and fun work climates. Much to my surprise, I only found support for the second half of my hypothesis. I learned there were ways to design environments that made work feel more fun, that prompted workers to express more enjoyment and happiness. The presence of fun coworkers was not predictive of this at all. In other words, enjoyment at work is not related to someone's personality or their mood—it's driven by the design of their organization.

To create meaningful, positive impacts, the levels of analysis that matter are not just individual, but also group and system. Yet could you not argue that the core question of organizing is how to ensure that any individual in an organization has the right information to make the right decisions at the right time (Dignan 2019)? Perhaps, but the challenge with considering interventions at the individual level in organization design is that you cannot actually change the individual. Sure, you can try to hire the right person with the right skills and the right attitude, and these are all good and important objectives. But once the person is within the organization's four walls, for the most part, you have what you have. Spending time teaching interpersonal communication skills, coaching for implicit bias, and investing in leadership development could bring about some change at the individual level in some cases, but ultimately, focusing on the individual is a flawed approach to changing an organization.

When we do try to positively influence the workforce, our interventions predominately focus on individuals—their skills, their mindsets, their strengths—yet there is ample evidence showing these tactics don't impact team effectiveness or organizational performance (Duhigg 2016). For example, the largest study ever done on teams, with the most data and computing power, was Project Aristotle by Google, which proved that individual attributes like personality (e.g., extroversion), intelligence (IQ), performance, seniority, tenure and so on had *no* impact on team performance (Duhigg 2016).

We have repeatedly restructured our traditional hierarchies and moved individuals around but have made minimal improvements because we were ignoring group and system dynamics. It is the networks of relationships at the team and at the organization level that show us how decisions get made and how work actually gets done, and ultimately how people behave.

Design Ignores the Power of Horizontal Networks

Organizations have traditionally been relentless in their pursuit of an ideal design that leads to maximized output, productivity, and stability. The problem is that almost every minute of the day geared toward these pursuits is dedicated to a relatively small percentage of what it takes to get things right. With recent advancements in the field of network analysis, it is becoming evident that important work is increasingly accomplished collaboratively through networks. But until very recently, the only network we ever paid attention to was the hierarchy.

Network analysis is a set of mathematical techniques to depict relations among people and to analyze the social structures that emerge from these relationships.

If you have heard of "spans and layers," "sticks and boxes," "dotted and solid lines," or ever seen an organization chart, you have been exposed to hierarchy. But this is only one type of network among many! And the formal structures underpinning organizational charts do not reflect the vast majority of the knowledge flows within organizations.

With the power of data and analytics, we can now make many types of networks visible, not just the traditional vertical hierarchy. There are at least six core layers of knowledge, each comprising its own informal network of people: work network, social network, innovation network, expert knowledge network, career guidance/ strategic network, and learning network.

According to social network theorist Karen Stephenson (Kleiner 2002), this means the hierarchical work network accounts for maybe 20% of knowledge in organizations, so we have, until now, ignored the other 80%. We have been hard at work improving the things that account for at most 20% of organizations' value and leaving at least 80% to chance. Even if it's not 80%, even if it's only 50%, just think of how much power we now have to improve how our organizations are designed if we look at *all* the networks, not just one.

Trust relationships and how they span across an organization can now be visualized using network analysis. Seeing them allows us to influence them, which enables us to transform the workplace—and by extension, work overall. In human networks, what matters is your distance in terms of your relationships. Are you connected to the right people? Do these connections include people who offer nonredundant sources of knowledge and wisdom? Are you stuck in an echo chamber of common thinking, also known as groupthink, or do you find yourself at the intersection of knowledge clusters where innovations happen?

Once you know your network, you can take action within your network because now there is a road map. You can make new connections between individuals and groups that need to exchange knowledge or translate understanding to move everyone forward with new discoveries or better implementation (Kleiner 2002). This cannot just be left to a few leaders who talk about a collaborative culture. It requires intentionally structuring the horizontal organization, just as we have historically structured the hierarchy.

But Are There Really Problems with How Organizations Are Currently Designed?

As my Lean Six Sigma teacher used to say, "In God we trust; all others bring data." So, let's start with some data. Between 55% and 80% of us do not enjoy work (Greater Good 2019). In addition, 85% of employees are disengaged, and 37% believe that their job makes no useful contribution to society (Minnaar and de Morree 2019). A Deloitte survey on workplace burnout reports that 77% of respondents say they have experienced burnout at their current job. Employees experiencing burnout are 63% more likely to call in sick and 2.6 times more likely to be looking for a new job (Wigert 2020). These figures all have a direct and profound impact on a company's bottom line.

Work as we know it today is simply not working. One reason for these dismal statistics is corporate bureaucracy. In their latest book, *Humanocracy*, Gary Hamel and Michele Zanini, the cofounders of the Management Lab, say that roughly half of the 23.8 million management roles in the United States are unnecessary (Hamel and Zanini 2020). For example, their data show that we waste approximately 16% of our working lives on internal administrative tasks.

Today's workplaces are broken. We face cumbersome internal mechanisms, antiquated procedures, and redundant, overlapping roles. Managers of complex organizations spend about 60% of their total work hours in coordination meetings, which are nothing more than working on work (Morieux and Tollman 2014). This gives them less time with their teams, and in turn, they spend up to 80% of their time working harder and harder on non-value-adding activities.

Our organizations are designed for efficiency, and our structure and human resource systems reinforce working within our own department or function, which taps into our natural tendency for homophily.

(*Homophily* is the tendency to form strong social connections with people who share one's defining characteristics, such as age, gender, ethnicity, socioeconomic status, and personal beliefs.) A silo mentality has a corrosive effect on culture by breeding distrust, conflict, resentment, and low morale. Executives surveyed in a 2017 McKinsey poll ranked siloed thinking and behavior as the *number 1* obstacle to a healthy organizational culture (Goran, LaBerge, and Srinivasan 2017).

We have focused on the strategies and capabilities needed to win in the market but ignored how these choices directly impact the ways in which workers themselves find a sense of meaning and belonging. If you were an artist painting a portrait, would you spend all of your time on just 20% of the canvas, leave the rest blank and hope that somehow a beautiful work of art would appear? Probably not. Unfortunately, that's what has been happening for far too long in the world of work.

Organizations need to intentionally intervene at the system and group level—not just the individual level—unifying all so they work in harmony, as a system. Using the principles of psychology, these designs and reorganizations need to be informed by how the human brain, with all its quirks, operates so that all workers consistently experience meaning, belonging, and mastery because these all have a direct and positive impact on the bottom line (as does having all aspects of organization design work in harmony). Organizations need to leverage the power of network science to purposefully structure networks of teams in ways that reduce friction and unleash collective intelligence instead of leaving almost everything to chance.

To shed light on how to move forward, I have combined industrial psychology, organization theory, behavioral economics, social science, network science, and current technological advances to create a view of the modern organization. My goal is to teach organizational leaders how to design organizations that get the business outcomes they want. I will show you a proven model that will allow organizations to focus on the *entire* canvas.

2

Solving the Right Problem

Organization designers are like architects for groups and systems in organizations—they must come into an environment, understand it, and change it for the better. Humans are intrinsically motivated, and knowing how we tick in social settings (like work) informs the architect to design the right conditions to encourage people to flourish at work. As Deming told us more than 50 years ago, the fact is the system that people work in and their interactions with people may account for 90% or 95% of performance.

A typical work environment is fraught with unclear scope of authority, misleading goals, agreement without cooperation, ineffective motivators, unclear decision rights, wrong information, and misleading structure. When we dig into the research on the common issues that make for an unhappy, unproductive workplace, what do we find?

9

- Lack of ownership
- Poor collaboration and overlap in roles
- Perception of pay and performance unfairness
- An us-versus-them mentality
- Lack of social connections
- Lack of empowerment and autonomy

Note that these are all group-level dynamics. They occur because we are hardwired to belong, but in today's organizations, the conditions that create that sense of belonging are suboptimal. This is critically important, so let's explore it further.

Lack of Ownership

"No bosses! No titles!" This kind of messaging accompanies an idealized organization chart, or org chart, that shows a series of concentric circles, a constellation of stars, or even a tree of life. The stories and anecdotes that circulate around this no-boss movement are usually about how small groups of peers self-organize—without the tyranny of managers—to create breakthrough results. Never mind the lack of accountability and clarity these types of changes create. Hierarchy is out, and self-organization is in.

However, when you look more closely for examples of this, it is impossible to find companies that actually self-organize. Sometimes we see fewer management layers. Sometimes we see teams that can decide how to organize their roles and resources to get specific outcomes accomplished. Sometimes these teams are able to set their own objectives and rewards. But all these teams exist within some defined hierarchy. When scholars attempt to find an organization that is not characterized by hierarchy, they cannot (Mochari 2014).

Yet many modern-day organizational theorists still hold the idea that "hierarchy = power = exploitation = evil" (Haidt 2012). Before coming to such conclusions, it's helpful to use a biological and an evolutionary psychology lens to understand how we as individuals view our groups and our environments.

Any evolutionary psychologist will tell you, hierarchy is forever. The desire to obtain status in organizational settings is, simply put, part of human nature (Nicholson 1998). Our brains evolved to be hardwired to know who was superior and who was subordinate so that we could increase our chances of survival. This literature has been reinforced by neurological researchers in studies that have shown different brain areas are activated when a person moves up or down in a pecking order. In fact, our brains are activated by a potential change in hierarchical status as much as they are winning money, reflecting its influential role in human motivation and health (National Institutes of Health 2008).

When decisions must be made quickly, when knowledge is concentrated at the top, and several business decisions need to be coordinated at the enterprise level, the value of hierarchy is evident (Dignan 2019). And let's not forget that upper management sets the rules that guide the types of self-organizing allowed to happen (Dignan 2019). In the end, hierarchy is the most efficient, hardiest, and most natural structure ever devised for large organizations, according to social scientist Elliott Jaques (1990). One of Jaques's great contributions was to describe the time horizons at each level of a hierarchy. His insight was that real hierarchical boundaries occur at spans of 3 months, 1 year, 2 years, 5 years, 10 years, and 20 years (Jaques 1990). Understanding the elegance of hierarchy and its simple ability to clarify accountability is a core part of this book.

The structure of traditional managerial oversight is often illustrated by an org chart, a diagram of the official hierarchy. This is the simplest view of an organizational reporting structure, diagramming both authority and communication flow. It's hard to imagine the org chart as an invention, but Daniel McCallum designed the first modern org chart in 1855 as a guide for the New York and Erie Railroad. (See Figure 2.1.)

In addition to revolutionizing management structure, McCallum wrote six principles for running a hierarchical organization. Most are what you expect regarding "proper division of responsibilities," but

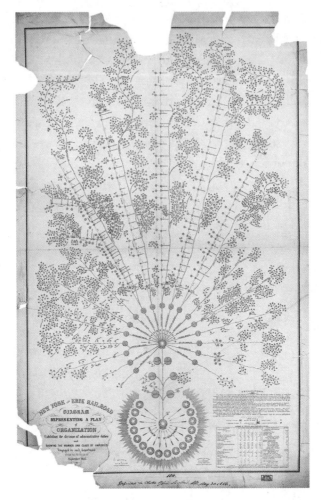

Figure 2.1   The first modern org chart was designed by Daniel McCallum and drafted by G.H. Henshaw.
Source: The Library of Congress

the fifth principle of the org chart is "to produce such information to be obtained through a system of reports and checks that will not embarrass principal officers nor lessen their influence with their subordinates."

If you have ever wondered why so much of what workers in large organizations know is shielded from the chief executive officer (CEO) and vice versa, wonder no longer! The idea of limiting communications so that they flow only from one layer of the hierarchy to the next was part of the system design at the dawn of the management culture (Jaques 1990). The challenges with how organizations are structured today will be further explored in the chapter on hierarchy.

Poor Collaboration and Overlapping Roles

Companies have been designed like machines. The engineering jargon we use to talk about organizations reveals how deeply we hold this metaphor. As corporate advisor and coach Frédéric Laloux says, "We talk about units and layers, inputs and outputs, efficiency and effectiveness, pulling the lever, moving the needle, acceleration and hitting the brakes. Changes must be planned and blueprinted, then carefully implemented. If some of the machinery functions below the expectation, it is probably time for some soft intervention and the occasional team building—like injecting oil to grease the wheels" (Laloux 2014, p. 28). However, adding a soft approach to grease the wheels does not make a happy organization. Both the hard and soft approaches seek to control the individual—the soft just assumes that what matters is emotional rather than financial stimuli. People feel bad and ineffective, so they get teambuilding and celebrations, but unfortunately only the symptoms have been addressed, not the underlying problems. As author and director of Boston Consulting Group's Institute for Organization, Yves Morieux, said in his TED Talk, "The effectiveness of the company is at the interplay, the interactions, the synapses. Not the skeleton of boxes, but the nervous system of intelligence. The real battle is not against competitors. The real battle is against ourselves" (Morieux 2014).

If the industrial economy was driven by economies of scale, the knowledge economy is driven by economies of networks. With the power of organization network analysis, we can thoughtfully develop designs that take network knowledge into account to help people clarify their roles to make better decisions and follow through on their intention to act. This will be further explained in Chapter 5: Networks.

Unfairness in Pay and Performance Measurement

Our brains are hardwired to seek fairness, which drives the concerns about equality and justice or the fear that those at the top of the organization gain by exploiting those at the bottom. This was a major theme of the Occupy Wall Street movement. Everyone cares about fairness, but there are two different kinds. One definition of fairness implies equality, but the other implies proportionality—people are rewarded in proportion to what they contribute, even if that guarantees unequal outcomes.

This principle makes us want to shun or punish cheaters. This provides evidence for the human instinct toward procedural justice at work. John Stacey Adams' equity theory explains that we are motivated when our perceptions of the workplace are fair and not when it's unfair (Adams 2020). What matters most in workplace motivation is the effort we put in and the outcomes we get. If we see it's fair, we will be motivated. Conversely, if you see a colleague doing the same work but getting paid more, or you see another colleague who has the same reward but seems to be doing less, you will probably lose your intrinsic motivation.

In Daniel H. Pink's book *Drive*, he writes at length about the difference between what science knows and what business does (Pink 2011). A good example of how business does the opposite of science can be found in performance appraisals. In many companies, collaboration and helping others isn't really in your own self-interest because you are competing with your teammates for annual reviews. In fact, NeuroLeadership Institute CEO David Rock's research shows that when we receive a rating or appraisal, our brain shifts into fight-or-flight mode and begins to rely on our limbic brain (Weller 2019). This shift, which takes place whenever we are threatened, immediately takes us out of the mode to learn or create, making us defensive. Ironically, the actual act of executing a performance appraisal itself reduces performance. We will explore this more fully in Chapter 7: Measurement.

Us-Versus-Them Mentality

Much of the us-versus-them dynamic has been eloquently described in social psychologist Jonathan Haidt's model of loyalty and betrayal. The loyalty/betrayal foundation in our brains evolved in response to the adaptive challenge of forming and maintaining coalitions (Haidt 2012). The foundation is just part of our innate preparation for meeting the adaptive challenge of forming cohesive coalitions. The trigger for this is anything that tells you who is a team player and who is a traitor, particularly when your team is fighting with other teams. Have you ever wondered why silo walls become so high and so thick so quickly? Once you self-identify with a group and become a member—let's say you work in the marketing department—you will show a robust bias toward your group. The marketing folks really "get" you, and you enjoy working together as professionals. Not like those salespeople. . . .

The love of loyal teammates is matched by a corresponding hatred of traitors, who are usually considered to be far worse than enemies. People reaching across groups can be seen as traitors or with suspicion. Who can forget *Romeo and Juliet* and the many other feuds and wars based around loyalty and identity? They show us how important and salient perceptions of group identity can be.

Given such strong links to love and hate, is it any wonder we see this foundation taking an important role in feelings of belonging within organizations and an equally important role in creating competition between groups? Think back to the example where we restructured a company from a focus on products to solutions and the ensuing tension, disagreement and actual infighting this created between sales, marketing and engineering. These dynamics will be further explored in Chapter 8: Membership.

Lack of Social Connection

Organization designers are keenly interested in social ties and relationships, so they study groups of people, whether large or small. Groups can be anything from a "two-pizza" project team to a department to a business unit or country made up of multiple departments to whole generations of people (think of millennials and all the attention they got as a group).

According to social neuroscience researchers, our human ancestors depended as much on social belonging for survival as they did on food and shelter. Poor social standing on both an individual and group basis can actually lead to a *higher mortality rate*. This explains why we are often "groupish" rather than selfish. We deploy our reasoning skills to support our team and demonstrate commitment to our team (Haidt 2012).

How can social connections possibly be lacking in our modern environment where almost all our work is done in collaboration with others? Our collaboration requirements have risen at least 50% in the last several years (Cross 2021). Think about how much more collaboration we are required to do today and the cost of that collaboration (e.g., the wasted time in meetings, wrong people in meetings, spending time talking with no decisions made, revisiting of decisions). According to network scientist Rob Cross (2021), collaboration today consumes 85% or more of our workweek. This collaboration overload has largely gone unchecked.

Social connections are essential to health and well-being, yet our current collaboration overload (Cross 2021) has resulted in unprecedented levels of stress and burnout at work. This is because we have arguably unsustainable patterns of connectivity, but this doesn't reflect the quality of our relationships. Social connection is really about connectedness: the extent to which we engage with important, supportive people in our lives in ways that heighten our sense of belonging and well-being.

Though the workplace is often perceived as a logical, transaction-based environment, it is still occupied by humans—and humans are emotional beings. When leaders implement any kind of change in an organization, they must consider the impact it will have on their people. Asking people to play multiple roles on different teams that often are incentivized and rewarded at cross-purposes requires more collaboration but with less quality connections.

Let's go back to our sales and marketing example. The executive team directed the two groups to collaborate more. Now salespeople were supposed to think beyond their one product line and customer base and partner with other sales folks to share customer insights and help their peers sell other products. They were asked to collaborate and team and do so with an enterprise mindset. Yet their group targets and individual goals were in direct competition with one another. Taking valuable time away from selling to customers to collaborate literally cost the salespeople money. Not only did it cost them money to help their peers, but it cost them more money to help marketing—and they didn't even like those marketing people!

Every time a person's social environment changes, it challenges their sense of stability by way of the brain's circuitry. And in today's world, with back-to-back 30-minute meetings each day, our social environment can change 16 times in 8 hours. If the brain decides the change is, in fact, threatening, then it will resist or avoid the change as much as possible—fight-or-flight mode. We will explore these collaboration challenges further in Chapter 10: Teaming.

Lack of Empowerment

Authority flows down and accountability flows up in the hierarchy. On the other hand, responsibility is something you feel is your duty, and you do it to increase trust within your networks. It means you do the things you are supposed to do. When you are irresponsible, you breed mistrust; when you are responsible, trustworthiness ensues. A person in a job with higher authority in the hierarchy can delegate accountability for outcomes. Whether you accept responsibility for this is up to you as an individual in your role or roles.

To understand the root of this, we can look at how our brains treat fairness and cheating, which centers on the idea of reciprocal altruism. It evolved in response to the adaptive challenge of reaping the rewards of cooperation without getting exploited. Suppose a coworker offers to take on your workload for 5 days so you can add a second week to your Caribbean vacation. How would you feel? It's a big favor, and you can't repay your coworker simply by bringing back a bottle of rum. If you accept the offer, you are likely to do so while gushing forth expressions of gratitude and a promise to do the same for her whenever she goes on vacation (Haidt 2012). You feel responsible.

Evolution created altruists in our species because we can remember prior interactions and limit our niceness to those who will likely repay a favor. We cooperate with those who have been nice to us, and we shun those who took advantage of us. According to social psychologist Jonathan Haidt (2012), "Human life is a series of opportunities for mutually beneficial cooperations. If we play our cards right, we can work with others to enlarge the pie that we ultimately share." The art, then, of architecting an effective and productive organization is the right mix of authority in the hierarchy and responsibility in the networks. We will explore this in Chapter 9: Responsibility.

3 | The Peopletecture Model

"Systems are not improved by tinkering with the parts, but by working on their interactions. It is not so much the parts that matter, but their fit."
— Niels Pfaegin, *Organize for Complexity* (2020)

Systems differ from groups in that they are considered a more formal and more organized way of collecting people together around specific goals and norms. Those of us who study organizations might also be interested in comparing similar organizations to reveal the nuanced ways in which they operate and the norms that shape those operations (Cole 2020). The opening quote describes how we are, once again, doing a great job fixing the wrong problem.

In *Thinking in Systems*, environmental scientist Donella Meadows (2008) describes what a system is, stating that a system "isn't just a collection of any old things, [it] is an interconnected set of elements that is coherently organized in a way that achieves something." She further defines a system as consisting of functions, interactions, and elements and goes on to describe how the components of a system are more than the sum of their parts.

The interconnections of a system occur through the flow of information, and this flow plays a predominant role in determining how a system operates (Meadows 2008). A system generally operates on being itself, changing only slowly if at all—even with complete substitutions of its elements—as long as its interconnections and purposes remain intact. If the interconnections change, the system may be greatly altered. It may even become unrecognizable, even though the same players are on the team. For instance, if you change the rules of a game from those of football to basketball, you've got, as they say, a whole new ballgame (Meadows 2008).

This perspective helps explain why so many "reorgs" don't seem to actually produce much more than new org charts and should give us pause when a new leader is eager to make changes by looking first at people, departments, or product lines. Putting different handles on faucets may change the look, but they're the same old faucets, plumbed into the same old system. These new handles will not change the quality of the water pressure or of the water itself. With the same old networks of information and goals and incentives, the system behavior isn't going to change much.

When companies look to design or redesign, they tend to look at only a few of the trade-offs. They make changes to only a subset of the variables that create the organizational context and affect individuals' and groups' experiences of being happy and productive. Self-described "leadership philosopher" Niels Pflaeging calls this the improvement paradox, where he illustrated that working on separate parts does not improve the whole, but instead actually damages it (Meadows 2008).

We cannot go from entangled to enlightened by single interventions, such as a team-building exercise. To implement change, we must design the whole system and understand the dynamics of the different layers of the organization based on the context we create. In other words, I feel the way I feel about you or your group not because of who you are but because we are parts, and if we integrated in some meaningful way, I would feel very differently about you or your group (Oshry 2018).

To summarize what we have covered so far, six key levers must be pulled, and they must be pulled at the same time in the same direction to get the best business outcomes:

- Hierarchy
- Networks
- Measurement
- Membership
- Responsibility
- Teaming

The *hierarchical* structures in organizations create a frame for our experiences at work. In this frame, we become *members* of a group where we feel a sense of belonging, and we learn to *team* effectively within social *networks* that influence our feelings about our work and our performance. We take *responsibility* for our part of the work that needs to be done, and expect our efforts to be *measured* fairly.

These six areas need to transform to address the fundamental challenges stated earlier—a lack of ownership, poor collaboration, and overlap in roles, perception of pay and performance unfairness, an us-versus-them mentality, lack of social connections, and a lack of empowerment and autonomy. See Table 3.1 for a summary.

The only way that groups of humans can arrive at a common course of action is by structuring interpersonal connections (Turchin 2020). This can be done vertically through hierarchy or horizontally through networks, and both of these dimensions can be supported by measuring in a way that provides the right conditions for motivation. We will talk more in-depth about each of these later in this book, examining what doesn't work and what small and larger adjustments can be made to create a more thriving, innovative, and ultimately profitable workplace for everyone.

You can design membership in groups, craft roles on teams, and support these designs with the right level of empowerment by allocating accountability in a way that allows teams to take responsibility for their work. Focusing on these factors directly impacts the

Table 3.1 Origins of the Peopletecture Model

Elements	Hierarchy	Networks	Measurement	Membership	Responsibility	Teaming
Source of	Identity: Where do I live?	Trust: Who helps me?	Mastery: How do I excel?	Belonging: Where do I fit in?	Autonomy: How am I empowered?	Growth: How do I develop?
Definition	Where the solid reporting lines are that denote the four "magic wands": hire, fire, pay, and promote	The informal structures that show how work is truly done and how much unnecessary friction exists	How incentives, performance management, and targets can be optimized for knowledge work in a way that is perceived as fair and that drives the right behaviors	How jobs are designed and managed in the hierarchy to create belonging and hold people and groups accountable	How and where decisions are made, when and by whom, and how clearly the decision roles and processes are communicated and followed	The multiple roles you will play in your networks and how you will work together to grow and develop

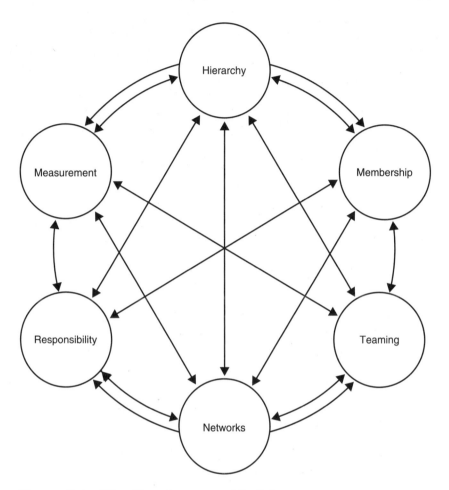

Figure 3.1   The Peopletecture Model

sense of belonging, mastery, and autonomy the workforce experiences. The focus is on creating context that meets the needs and wants of the individual actor in multiple roles.

Figure 3.1 highlights the Peopletecture Model, showing how creating a workplace in which individuals feel fulfilled actually starts by focusing on groups more than individuals.

The six elements (hierarchy, networks, measurements, member-ship, responsibility, and teaming) are wired into our brains. They developed over the history of our species to address adaptive challenges. We have both the research and real-world understanding of all these elements and how they operate together as one system, and now we can apply the insights to the six underlying challenges today's organizations face.

4

Hierarchy

"Change does not come by fixing, firing, replacing, or retraining
the people, but rather it comes from changing the pattern."
— Barry Oshry, *Context, Context, Context* (2018)

Hierarchy still dominates the thinking of top-level executives in the
largest organizations in the world. One story from early in my
consulting career will help provide some context into just how
bogged down in hierarchy companies can become when struggling
with important decisions.

It was hour three of an all-day executive committee meeting.
After facilitating the team through some challenging decisions on
how to transform their health system to be better positioned for the
market shift that would reward health outcomes instead of patient
volume, they decided on center-led corporate functions that would
support the markets.

In this case, they had decided to make region their primary axis
for the hierarchy, and traditional support functions like human
resources and finance were to be shared across the regions. We had
arrived at the part of the day where we began to discuss the
organizational architecture that would best deliver value to their
patients and their care workers. My favorite part!

Or so I thought.

An hour goes by. Then two. Fast forward to hour four. Then five. The chief finance officer (CFO) and the chief human resources officer (CHRO) were intently engaged in a heated debate that began before lunch and was still going strong. The question on the table seemed deceptively simple: "There are corporate teams and regional teams. In order to encourage collaboration, should these teams have a solid-line reporting into the center and a dotted-line reporting into the region, should it be the opposite, or should there be *two* solid lines, one to the region and one to the center?"

As it went on and on and became more and more heated and seemingly adversarial, I was like a dog at a tennis match. I looked right, then left, right, left. All I could think about was that one of *my* central missions was to, once again, facilitate my clients toward a solution. At that point, it seemed that all I was doing was sitting in a car that was quickly approaching a brick wall.

I kept trying to steer the conversation back on course, but it simply was not working. My opening suggestion had been to pick only one reporting relationship to keep the chain of command in the hierarchy clear. This was met with instant and harsh criticism from the CFO.

"I need all the finance people reporting directly to me!" he exclaimed. My team looked uncomfortable. For me, uncomfortable would've been a marked improvement. The rest of the executives shifted in their chairs, looking down or away. We've all been in meetings during *those* moments. This was one of those moments.

I tried to bring evidence to my recommendation. "Let me explain: Matrix reporting takes a toll on people by harboring ambiguity and unclear expectations. Each is the enemy of employee engagement. Gallup research indicates that clarity of expectations is a foundation for building an engaged workplace that performs at high levels. A matrix structure gives rise to a lack of clarity about responsibilities, expectations, and to whom they report."

The CHRO tried to help me. It was like a life preserver appearing in the middle of a stormy ocean. She described a series of meetings—finance meetings with the direct-line manager (in this case, the CFO) and regional meetings with the matrix manager. The agendas, objectives, and results sounded like they were from two different organizations. It was clear there was a problem that needed attention.

Unfortunately, the CFO didn't seem to care about how people felt working in this toxic arrangement, only that he had control over his legacy resources. Despite my pleas and those of the CHRO, we were in the throes of real-life sticking points about decision rights: who has them and who merely influences. Understanding who affects versus who ultimately controls compensation, ratings, and career advancement is always top of mind for executives.

We'll get back to how we resolved this quagmire in a bit. In the meantime, perhaps you can relate to having two managers. This design implies that each employee will have a different goal or goals defined by each manager. Now, if you imagine that in a team of seven everyone has two goals, this means we have 14 individual goals that have nothing to do with the team goal, which is the most important one.

Of course, you can say the team as a whole will have its goal and all the individual goals will end up aligned with the team goal, but do you believe that with so many different managers, different people, and different goals that people will be fully aligned with the team goals? Hardly. Roles and accountabilities are often confused, which creates friction and destroys trust.

Everyone should be focused on building a better hierarchy. Real power is in understanding this, because once we do, we can assess the existing problems in the design and make real and lasting changes that allow us to create our desired future—realizing our full potential at work.

Hierarchies Are Necessary

Hierarchy is not only an organizing principle in business; it is also one of the foundations of the very biological system in which all organisms exist. Why? It has a lot to do with the cost of connection. If it were possible to have a network without connection costs, organisms in nature would *not* evolve to be hierarchical. That's not how it works in our ecosystem or in the modern world of organizations. Whenever connection costs are present, our neurons evolve toward a hierarchical bent with an innate focus on making connections.

That innate focus continuously impacts organizations. Every transaction an organization undertakes, every contract, every agreement, every meeting requires expending one or more resources that are finite and limited in nature. These include not just money, but time and *attention*. As a result, no organization can put all its energies into pursuing its mission. Instead, it must expend considerable effort maintaining discipline and structures simply to keep itself viable (Shirky 2008).

Hierarchy is a natural structure for large organizations. As Elliott Jaques (1990) said after 35 years of management research, "Properly structured, hierarchy can release energy and creativity, rationalize productivity, and actually improve morale." Many recent management trends have attempted "flatter" hierarchies in an attempt to react to market forces more quickly, like a startup might. However, they have been bewildered to find that their flatter hierarchies do not create speed—because fewer empowered decision-makers resulted in decision bottlenecks, which actually slows things down further. But what do we mean when we say "flat"?

Different Structures

Organizations have a choice when it comes to hierarchy in terms of whether they prefer one that is "flat" or one that is "tall." That choice will have a profound impact on employee and manager efficiency and effectiveness. For example, conventional military structure is vertical, but radical groups typically use flat structure with decentralized control and communications, as was characterized in *Team of Teams* by General Stanley McChrystal (2015).

Compare these two different org charts in Figure 4.1 for a flat company (on the right) with only two levels and a vertical company

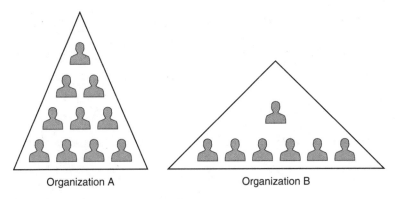

Organization A   Organization B

Figure 4.1   Tall versus flat.

Source: Levitin, 2015 / Penguin Publishing Group

(on the left) with four levels. The command structure in corporate and military organizations can take either form, and each system has advantages and disadvantages.

A flat structure has advantages. A flat structure encourages people to work together and allows for overlap in effort, often empowering employees to do what needs to be done and apply their talents outside of formal command or task structure.

A drawback of flat structures is that only one person might have effective decision-making authority and that person will have too many decisions to make. Due to the lack of a hierarchy, extra effort is needed to establish who is accountable for which tasks. *Some* form of vertical structure is essential to achieve coordination among employees and their projects to avoid duplicate effort and to coordinate across different components of a project.

Tall vertical systems usually encourage specialization and the efficiencies that come from it. Workers tend to fully understand the scope of their role in this structure and generally can execute the tasks they know they own without hesitation or confusion. There is less risk for overlap in a vertical system.

However, tall structures can also result in employees being isolated from one another and working in silos, unaware of what others are doing that might be closely related to their own work. When a vertical system becomes too tall, meaning it contains too many levels, it can take too much time for instructions to filter down to the ground from higher up or for crucial information from lower levels to reach the top (Levitin 2015). These same descriptions of structure—flat or vertical—can be applied to any website, as Daniel Levitin (2015) shows in *The Organized Mind*. We all navigate our way through websites, and we all understand how differently they can be built and organized.

Imagine that the previous flat and vertical structure drawings are sitemaps for two different versions of a company's website. Both websites will present visitors with the exact same data, but the visitors' experiences will be vastly different within these different structures. With a well-designed flat navigation, the visitor can obtain summary information in one click and more detailed information in two clicks (Levitin 2015).

With vertical navigation, that same visitor might find summary information in one or two clicks, but the detailed information will require four clicks. Of course, websites aren't always designed well or in a way that allows a visitor to find what they're looking for. Hence the user may end up doing a great deal of searching, fishing, and backtracking. The flat organization makes it easier to backtrack, while the vertical structure makes it easier to locate a hard-to-find file if the visitor can be sure they're in the correct subnode (Levitin 2015).

Still, there are limits to flat organizations' ease of use: If the number of middle-level categories becomes too great, it takes too long to review them all, and because they themselves are not hierarchically organized, there can be redundancies and overlap. Much the same, website visitors can easily become overwhelmed by too many choices—deep hierarchy offers fewer choices at once (Levitin 2015).

In a business setting, uncertainty about the chain of command when there's a problem can cause a situation to spiral out of control quickly. A small problem can explode into something extremely problematic. In this sense, organizations have an interest in curtailing this possibility. It could be chaotic if every employee were wandering around trying to find someone with answers every time they had a question.

To keep business running smoothly, companies rely on the chain of command, where each employee knows who is in charge, from the top position all the way down to the newest intern. Hierarchy undeniably has its drawbacks, challenged with how to release and sustain the initiative and adaptability of the entrepreneur. But it is the only form that can enable large numbers of people to have unambiguous accountability for their work (Jaques 1990).

With the rapidly changing environment and increasing uncertainty that professional teams face in the twenty-first century, organizations are looking to adopt structures that emphasize flexibility and quick response to change. These organizations may have flatter hierarchies and communication and decision-making patterns that do not fully adhere to the chain-of-command or unity-of-command principles, what is known as the "matrix" structure (Weber 2022).

In matrix organizations, employees frequently have two managers or supervisors. For example, a line employee reports to both a functional manager (e.g., the director of engineering) *and* a regional manager (e.g., the head of operations for Asia) in order to deliver a product or service in multiple locations with input from multiple functions. Right away you can see this violates the unity-of-command and chain-of-command principles.

By removing dotted-line reporting in the hierarchy and ensuring that only one person is accountable for any given set of leadership responsibilities, we can stop forcing employees to answer to multiple bosses who think it is within their purview to perform the same set of leadership functions, such as hiring and firing, promotions, and incentives. I have often referred to these four external motivators as the four magic wands of "hire, fire, pay, promote."

As we will see in the next chapter, Networks, there is a better way to preserve unity of command, reduce tension, increase speed and flexibility, and more effectively confront the challenges the matrix was meant to address in the first place (De Smet, Kleinman, and Weerda 2019).

The Silo Trap

According to team management expert Patrick Lencioni (2006), silos are nothing more than the barriers that exist between departments within an organization, causing people who are supposed to be on the same team to work against one another. To address any of the negative impacts of silos, leaders must go beyond behaviors and address the contextual issues at the heart of the departmental separation and politics.

Management at the top develops a strategy, and each functional unit *should* then implement this strategy. However, usually each unit ends up developing its own objectives, plans, metrics, etc. This results in what is termed the "silo effect." It means that every hierarchical unit sets its own priorities to fulfill its objectives, often resulting in a divergence of effort.

This also illustrates the pyramidic nature of the hierarchy, where work is divided up among different functions to the highest levels of the hierarchy and allocated to specialized activities among the lower layers. As a consequence of these hierarchical and functional barriers, operative islands emerge (Figure 4.2).

As we rise up through the organization, each respective layer's role increases in time frames and, therefore, complexity. By operating in this way, we ensure that the day-to-day activities are completed and that the higher layers of the organization are looking out over longer time frames to lead the way into the future.

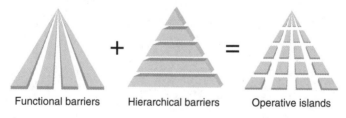

Functional barriers   Hierarchical barriers   Operative islands

Figure 4.2   Functional and hierarchical barriers lead to operative islands.

Source: Hörrmann and Tiby (1991) / G Hörrmann

A large corporation with thousands or tens of thousands of employees needs to be able to identify authority and accountability at each stage of the value-adding process, place people with the necessary competence at each stage, and build acceptance of the structure that achieves these ends (Jaques 1990).

However, when the work is broken out into specialized tasks by role, this can lead to disintegration of the natural flow of work, leading to a growing number of interfaces needed and increased coordination effort. Silos are not necessarily bad, and they are not a fault of leadership or a lack of a collaborative mindset, but they can waste resources, kill productivity, and jeopardize the achievement of enterprise goals.

To work effectively, each layer in the structure must be adding value, thereby reducing complexity and speeding up decision-making (Galbraith 2014). Formal structure is most useful when it defines the space of potential collaborators through organizational boundaries. That means that it encourages but also discourages interactions. This suggests that silos can actually be useful by containing the space.

Benefits of Hierarchy

Hierarchies are not always problematic. We have explored reasons that they came to be and why they still exist. Proper, strategic applications of a hierarchy can help an organization advance its core mission. For instance, a hierarchical structure with clear departmental boundaries, clean lines of authority, detailed reporting mechanisms, and formal decision-making procedures is particularly well-suited for mass production. The requirements of high-volume, high-speed operations demand the constant attention of a managerial team.

The strength of a hierarchical organization in this space depends upon its reliability. After all, such an organization's customers must rely on its capacity for producing large numbers of goods or services of a given quality repeatedly. It must also be able to foster an environment of accountability and be able to document how resources have been used (Hannan and Freeman 1984).

Hierarchy can be thought of as a vertical structure, but also as an underlying grid, from which all sorts of horizontal structures can emerge: self-organizing teams, mission-based teams, purpose-driven teams, project teams, scrum teams, agile teams, and innovation teams. Whether these horizontal structures are temporary or permanent, they can be formed around any mission or strategy or purpose, and with the right empowerment and metric design, they will thrive.

These structures form and dissolve around problems, needs, and goals. They are fluid and open. The function of hierarchy is then not to dominate others with damaging statements, such as, "I am the vice president, so my opinion is more important," but rather to hold the space for people to feel safe to work in these horizontal structures.

Even if the rules are clear in the network, sometimes you need an arbitrator with formal power. Imagine a youth soccer game without a referee or a coach, and it's not hard to see how it would become unruly and unfair quickly. The hierarchy is like the referee. A good referee does not dominate the game but provides and holds the space for fluid networks of teams. It performs as it should without really being noticed (Culen 2017).

The concept of vertical leverage (FAQs for Organizations 2016) comes from the layers of an organization that provide the leverage to produce a result that is greater than the sum of the parts. In addition to standardized workflows, such as risk, compliance, finance, and technology infrastructure, the more senior layers in the company should be accountable for:

- Providing the purpose and value of the organization
- Scanning the horizon to be aware of possible future circumstances
- Creating effective structures that enable the horizontal workflow
- Working with employees to implement better work practices
- Fixing issues
- Removing roadblocks
- Sharing resources, expenses and capital
- Brand management and recognition

A New Approach

Let's go back to my tense (and intense) meeting discussed at the opening of this chapter. At the end of what became a very long day, we came to a compromise. We landed on solid lines to the center and dotted lines to the region, meaning the central leader had the four magic wands: hire, fire, pay, and promote. While this was better than two solid lines, it was not what I aspired to achieve.

Yet, to be fair, to implement a new approach, top management must have a lot of confidence in their people and delegate the majority of their decision authority to the accountable teams. Until now, we have not had the ability to leverage the power of network insights to allow us to keep the hierarchy simple and efficient so we can spend the vast majority of our time working on architecting the right networks of teams and allowing them the autonomy to succeed. We will explore this in the next chapter, Networks.

This is the essence of the ongoing challenge. Hierarchy tells us that we should report to one and only one position in order to prevent conflicting orders. It also tells us we should have the fewest number of levels possible. In other words, only one solid line, not dotted, and the structure overall should be as flat as possible.

Anything that is explicit, that is transactional, that is done repeatedly but that cannot be automated goes here. The primary job of the leaders in the hierarchy is to enable horizontal flow. This is first done by delegating decision authority for the majority of decisions so that the reports in the hierarchy have clear accountability for their position in the vertical structure. This allows the teams to enter into reciprocal workflow relationships with members outside of their primary group and to hold each other responsible.

Let's take a set of human resources capabilities as an example. One of my clients broke out their human resources unit into a few subcapabilities: the talent shop, attraction, rewards, performance, well-being, analytics, and mastery—all grouped in terms of experts and resources. Members of each of these groups, whether you call them tribes like this company did, or departments like a more traditional company, derived a sense of identity from belonging to a group. They tend to be like minded in their profession, sharing mental models of both how to do the work and how to work together. They followed a set of company and industry best practices, professional standards, and policies for when they need to seek approval and what compliance and risk standards they must follow.

These folks reported in the hierarchy to one leader, the chief people officer, and they had clear decision authority over the topics in which they were experts. The rest of their work—and the majority of their time—occurred horizontally, on business teams that needed their capability. Their role was to bring their expertise to the business they supported. They didn't have "dotted-line" accountability to the businesses, just like we don't have dotted-line responsibility to our external customers. We still understand how we are accountable for delivering our services in the best way we can.

This is an example of a hierarchy done right; it gave people within a function a shared mental model that was nearly automated on an inherent level. That's what organizations should strive to achieve. If they do, they'll then be able to put much more of their focus where it is most effective, which is teaming horizontally with other functions to deliver business value.

5 | Networks

"There is a central difference between the old and new economies:
the old industrial economy was driven by economies of scale; the
new information economy is driven by the economics of networks."
—Carl Shapiro and Hal. R Varian, *Information Rules: A
Strategic Guide to the Network Economy* (1998)

I was hired by the president of a large health system a few years ago
to help her scale and spread their best practices. At the start of our
three-year journey together, some of her hospitals were performing
very well in terms of quality outcomes and patient satisfactions, while
others were performing dismally.

The differences in the performance were literally a matter of life
and death. Errors in a hospital setting lead to "adverse events," which
sounds relatively innocuous, but an adverse event can lead to patient
deaths. We needed to figure this out stat!

She had more than 20 hospitals spread out over two states, so to
get them all to operate consistently at the highest level of performance
was no small task. She was also very interested in innovation and
scaling up the pockets of great ideas and processes that existed in her
different hospital locations. This leader was clearly bright and curious.
She had already tasked a team of her best people to figure out why
some hospitals—even some floors of the *same* hospital—were over- or

under-performing in such significant ways. She had also tried in vain to scale some of the best innovations coming out of a single hospital to the rest of her hospitals.

She had compared the structure of the departments and the leadership skills of the executives of each hospital. She had looked at the number and type of doctors and nurses on staff. There were no real differences. In other words, there was no obvious or even relatively identifiable solution. She had a group of strong individual leaders running teams of basically similar size with degrees and experiences that looked pretty much the same. She had limited success and was frustrated and stuck. That's when I got the call.

As an innovator, my client was open to trying new things and willing to do whatever it took to protect the well-being of patients. So, as we set about to understand the current state, we first looked at the information she and her team had already examined. This included all the usual starting points: organization charts, process maps, policy and procedure documents, performance metrics, talent profiles, etc.

Then, we looked at the networks within each of the hospitals. More on what we figured out later, but suffice to say that the key was in the communication between and effectiveness of the various networks within the hospital.

The Nature of Networks

Organization charts show reporting hierarchy very well, but they don't show how coworkers interact with one another, and although they tell us about the formal relationships, they do not show informal relationships. Yet it is in the informal networks of relationships in an organization where most of the learning and work gets done and where all tacit knowledge gets exchanged. An organization comprises interconnected people, and they don't always conform well to organization charts.

Until recently, these connections have largely been intangible, which makes them difficult to plot on any type of chart or map. Yet most knowledge is exchanged in these networks. We have only focused on building better hierarchies and the enablers of human capital in organization design. We have been missing almost everything—until now.

The greatest opportunity for the future of organizations is to design horizontal or lateral structure.

Organization Network Analysis

Far from being the opposite of a network, hierarchies are just a special kind of network. Just as the organization chart provides a view of the formal structure of an organization, organization network analysis (ONA) provides a much-needed means to identify and visualize the informal networks within an organization. It reveals the various dimensions of networks through graphical representations that identify and show the relationships within those networks. Through ONA, organizations can start to understand the individual and collective relationships in the networks and their implications for the organization (McDowell 2016). Understanding, for example, how news is spread in a social network of people boils down to how a person's position in the network determines their influencing power and how their behaviors influence each other (Jackson 2019). Analysts use different algorithms to farm insights into a person's network, particularly to predict someone's behavior. What's really happening here is that network scientists are attempting to evaluate the centrality of a personal network. The centrality of people matters in how influential they are in steering other people's eventual beliefs. To understand the power of networks, let's look at how the Google algorithm works. In the Google algorithm, one does not judge a page simply by how many pages link to it, but also by whether it is linked to by well-connected pages.

In search engine parlance, the quality of the connections to a particular website is a central variable in determining what is known as "domain authority." Domain authority, in its most basic sense, is a numerical score—almost like a credit score—that helps define the trustworthiness and overall quality of a website. In essence, the domain authority of a website, based in large part on the quality of its connections, will help determine how many people will find that website at the top of their search returns when they are looking for something on Google.

How does this relate to organizational networks? The analogy is quite direct. In many cases, it is more important for a member of an organization to have well-connected friends than just to have many friends (Jackson 2019).

In business settings, being well-positioned makes one more attractive to attach to *and* easier to find, and the multiplier effect can be strong. Studying these structures can provide essential insights into influence. The greater the role the network has in the formation of new relationships, the greater the compounding effect and the resulting inequality in connectedness (Jackson 2019). You can imagine how this has important implications not just for organization design but also for understanding diversity and inclusion, retention and succession, culture and experience, and many other critical factors in the life of an organization.

One example of this is onboarding. A large oil and gas company had an ongoing campaign to hire the best and brightest engineers in the market. It brought this top talent in regularly, and over 4 years it managed to get these premium resources to be fully productive: as productive as those with 5 or more years of tenure. One innovative human resources analytics person studied these new hires over several years using network analysis. They had good cost and revenue data on the difference between a new engineer compared to a tenured resource. With this, they were able to demonstrate the business value of accelerating time to productivity. They showed that by understanding the work networks of those successful, tenured engineers, and deliberately structuring the new hires' relationships to mimic these, the time to productivity dropped from four years to six months.

We all know our own networks, but we don't know the details of other people's networks. We can only see our own networks, so we can be fooled by our egocentric network view. The reality of the situation, though, is that you are in an ocean of interpersonal connections, helping shape who you are, how you are trusted and how you trust others.

Network Roles

To better understand what network roles predict what types of behaviors, some researchers have used the following three categories (see Figure 5.1):

Hubs—Hubs are people who are socially connected to the *n*th degree. They have the highest number of direct ties to others and hold numerous face-to-face conversations, like the center of a star in a classic hub-and-spoke system. They are also effective multi-taskers who can juggle many activities, concepts, and relationships. Hubs are central. They can create a movement. They can change the majority of an organization's behavior! But you have to be careful what you say to Hubs. Although they are not likely malicious, they are so connected that any message may be quickly spread, and if it's a negative one, it will be potentially damaging, much in the same way a child unwittingly causes embarrassment by speaking the unadorned truth.

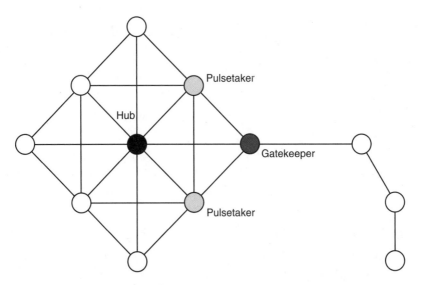

Figure 5.1   An example of human network strategies.

Source: Stephenson (2005) / Karen Stephenson

Gatekeepers—Gatekeepers serve as important links or bridges within an organization, functioning as human traffic directors on critical pathways between parts of an organization or between Hubs. When information must funnel through one person on the way to another, a Gatekeeper is the conduit, brokering the knowledge between Hubs. If this person likes you or the change the organization is trying to bring about, they can act as a valuable broker. Conversely, if the Gatekeeper does not support you or the change, they can slow down your progress by withholding critical information, becoming the proverbial "bottleneck." Because Gatekeepers do not have as many activities to juggle, they have more time to survey the political landscape.

Pulsetakers—Pulsetakers are connected through a great number of indirect ties. They are almost the opposites of Hubs in that they are unseen but all-seeing. Such people carry a lot of influence, much of it subtle. They are well versed in the culture of an organization, and an appreciable number of them evolve into great leaders. They are key to knowledge succession and, at the very least, should serve as mentors and coaches for the newly hired and uninitiated. A great historical example of a Pulsetaker is Machiavelli, who observed court intrigue and influenced it masterfully without a prominent station. In the more modern example of Silicon Valley, these are the "prairie dogs"—the ones who stick their head up over the cubicle wall every time they hear something interesting going on (Stephenson 2005, p. 247).

These are three types of roles at the nexus of knowledge within a network. And they transmit information amid a web of relationships using the powerful, cementing force of trust. Often, these different roles are summarized by practitioners to be the "influencers" in the network, those who can reach most of the population, influence their behavior, and drive adoption of a new product, technology, or idea. How do networks look and work in action? There are several different ways to measure them. Common network phenomena are defined by the following terms both for an individual and an organization as a whole, including small world, echo chambers, homophily, and bridging capital.

Small World

All humanity is connected (see Figure 5.2). As Stanley Milgram famously showed as far back as 1967, a maximum of six degrees of separation exists between you and any other person in the United States (Milgram 1967). This is known as the "small-world" phenomenon, made popular by the short story and later the play *Six Degrees of Separation* (Fass, Ginelli, and Turtle 1996) and more recently the game "Six Degrees of Kevin Bacon," where Kevin is always fewer than six connections away from everyone in Hollywood.

With the advent of the internet and global social networks like Facebook, that number may be even lower—as low as three-and-a-half degrees, according to a study conducted by Facebook in 2016 (Bhagat, Burke, and Diuk 2016). This is yet another way that the internet has made the world a smaller place.

Small-world networks have two characteristics that, when balanced properly, let messages move through the network effectively. The first is that small groups are densely connected. In a small group, the best pattern of communication is to connect with everyone.

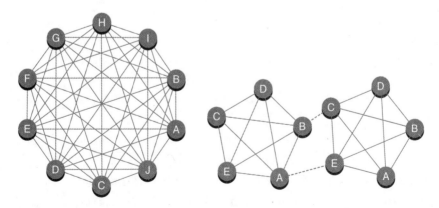

Figure 5.2   Different ways of connecting 10 people.

Source: Shirky (2008) / Penguin Publishing Group

In a network of five people, there would be 10 connections. If someone drops out, the other links would not be disrupted.

The second characteristic in small-world networks is that large groups are sparsely connected. As a leader, it is best to embrace both realities—let the small groups connect tightly and connect the groups. That said, you can't really connect groups, but rather you connect people within these groups (see Figure 5.3).

In the second image, instead of one loose group of 25, you have five tightly connected groups of five. As long as a couple of people in each group know a couple of people in other groups, you can have the advantages of a tight connection at a small scale and a loose connection at a large scale.

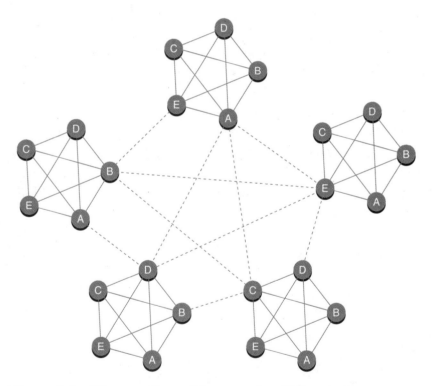

Figure 5.3   The small-world network of 25 people.

Source: Shirky (2008) / Penguin Publishing Group

If this is achieved, networks will be efficient and robust. A small world cheats nature by providing a better-than-random trade-off between the number of links required to connect a network and that network's effectiveness in relaying messages. These networks occupy a sweet spot between the unbuildable and the unusable, and as a side effect, they are highly resistant to damage (Shirky 2008).

Malcolm Gladwell made this famous in *The Tipping Point*, calling these "people connectors" (which in our earlier definition we called Gatekeepers) (Gladwell 2002). Conversely, in a strict, vertical hierarchy, almost everyone is a critical hub, since the loss of one person's connection disrupts communication to everyone connected through that person. A handful of people are extremely critical to holding the whole network together because, as the network grows, the existence of a small number of highly connected individuals enables the trade-off between connectivity and effectiveness.

Echo Chambers and Double Counting

Certain network structures can lead to repetitive information. In highly clustered networks, there is a plethora of chances for the same information to reach someone via multiple paths. We are constrained by information sets in our networks. This can become a problem on several levels.

This constraint is especially a problem when considering that we also have behavioral biases, including one called "correlation neglect." For instance, assume seven connections tell you the same thing, and you treat it as seven independent inputs; in reality, however, you're only hearing one input seven times.

Researchers have conducted many scientific experiments to demonstrate people double count and fail to rule out echoes of their own influence. For example, an experiment that has been repeated multiple times, called DeGroot learning, is amazingly predictive of how people's beliefs evolve (Jackson 2019). In this experiment, researchers put people into networks and assigned whom each person could talk to, so the experimenters could track what information came from which person. (Note: This is much like how we use hierarchy in organizations to control the flow of information in the network!) The results repeatedly illustrate that we all experience echoes and double counting and pay attention to people whose information might not be relevant.

So, can we structure a network to aggregate information accurately through our networks and not fall prey to bias? Well, if a group or an organization or a society does not have the right information among its members to begin with, it has no chance. But if we do have diversity of views that when averaged are accurate, then the other condition is that the network needs to be balanced. The unbalanced and centralized networks end up with biased opinions. See Figure 5.4.

Here we see a visual example of a balanced network versus an unbalanced network. Unbalanced information passes through a single person, and this person's own opinion will be reflected back in the final beliefs. This saves on communication costs but can easily end up with a biased opinion. This knowledge becomes incredibly important when we look to intervene in networks. Knowing how to balance a network to get good information in an organization becomes a huge competitive advantage that, until now, has been untapped.

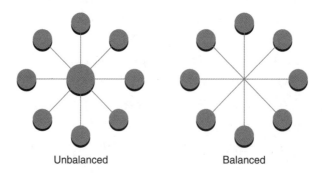

Unbalanced   Balanced

Figure 5.4   Unbalanced versus balanced network.
Source: Shirky (2008) / Penguin Publishing Group

Social media influencers are a prime example of society relying heavily on one person's opinion, and this happens in organizations too. Similarly, in an organizational setting, people who have many friends have their opinions leveraged by more people. This process has some important biases. There may be echoes present when your own opinion gets reflected back at you. For example, let's say you are one of the most popular people in the sales department and a Hub in this network. You hear that marketing was criticizing your department for slow sales despite their excellent marketing campaign. You are annoyed, and you complain to several of your sales colleagues. Later you speak to some sales folks from a different region, and you hear the same thing! But is this really independent information?

Actually, it is double counting, which is even more prevalent than the echo effect. You are getting opinions through two different channels because they shared that information between two regions, so it appears to be more reliable than if you hear it from the original sources, even when they are just relaying the same information—the information that you yourself communicated.

As a result of this unbalanced network full of echoes and double counting, you end up becoming overconfident as your sales friends confirm your beliefs. Now you're *really* mad at marketing! How dare those people!

Homophily

"Homo" refers to similarity and "phili" to love or fondness (Jackson 2019). People generally tend to interact with and live near others who are similar to themselves. For example, the co-locating of a highly educated population is a not-so-secret secret of the success of Silicon Valley.

Community boundaries are important in allowing us to cooperate and trust each other in our everyday lives. Repeated interactions allow us to reciprocate with people who help us and reprove detrimental behaviors. We build our work networks around our functions, professions, and other common features at work that put us into more frequent and well-defined contact with each other. Homophily reinforces itself. People can better predict the behaviors and reactions of those close to them (Jackson 2019).

Homophily is so fundamental to human networks and we are so familiar with it that it fades into the background. Forgetting about these basic network divides can lead people to propose ineffective policies when trying to fix such problems. Divisions in networks—and homophily in particular—can lead to persistent difference in beliefs and norms across groups. The human ability to grasp abstract concepts, enabling us to learn from each other and to coordinate our activities, is a double-edged sword. We rely on what we have heard from trusted resources. This allows the dramatic and persistent polarization that we see in people's beliefs on questions of fact.

Our understanding of homophily would also be incomplete if we failed to account for competition between groups. As researcher Mathew Jackson (2019) said, "How one person treats another involves looking beyond that relationship to the network in which they are embedded."

How do homophily and echo chamber insights help us think about silos and how they form? Let's go back to our classic example of sales and marketing. Sales dislikes marketing; marketing dislikes sales. Now we know it's because of network phenomena. *It was only one person who said only one thing, but the echo chambers make it seem like a hard fact that everyone is repeating.*

In addition, salespeople spend time together focused on the same things, doing the same things, so they really get each other. And the more time the salespeople spend with each other, the more homophily. The same goes for marketing, ultimately resulting in the two groups spending more time competing with each other internally than they do working together to win market share.

Our organizations are designed for efficiency, and our structure and human resource systems reinforce working within our own department or function, which taps into our natural tendency for homophily. Many authors say a silo mentality has a corrosive effect on culture by breeding distrust, conflict, resentment, and low morale. Executives in a 2017 McKinsey survey ranked siloed thinking and behavior as the number-one obstacle to a healthy organizational culture (Goran, LaBerge, and Srinivasan 2017). While not all silos are bad for all companies, an understanding of homophily does illuminate why our silos are so entrenched and difficult to overcome. But there are ways to restructure the network to overcome these dynamics of unbalanced networks, bias, and echo chambers, namely bridging.

Bridging Capital

In the renowned paper, *The Social Origins of Good Ideas*, sociologist Ronald Burt (2004) demonstrated in his research that most good ideas come from people bridging "structural holes," which is another way to describe people whose immediate work social networks include employees outside their department. Bridging these holes was valuable—bridging predicted good ideas, and a lack of bridging predicted bad ones. This finding is most likely true due to both homophily and echoes. Burt also found the network position predicted good ideas much more than any individual traits or skills (Shirky 2008).

Burt (2004) concluded, "People whose networks span structural holes have early access to diverse, often contradictory, information and interpretations which give them a good competitive advantage in delivering good ideas. People connected to groups beyond their own can expect to find themselves delivering valuable ideas, seeming to be gifted with creativity. This is not creativity born of deep intellectual ability. It is creativity as an import-export business."

Social Capital Benefits

Social relations can develop trustworthiness, but social relations have many other functions, including easing the exchange of fine-grained information (Uzzi 1997), gaining access to new information (Burt 1992), and enhancing power (Brass 1984). These functions have implications for organizational performance, individual well-being, and social welfare. Social relations become social capital when they have the potential to mobilize resources for individual or collective purposes (Lin 2001).

Burt found through numerous studies that certain patterns of connections that individuals build with others bring them higher pay, earlier promotions, greater influence, better ideas, and overall greater career success. He believes that good social capital provides a much higher return on investment in human capital—the two work together (Burt 1992).

In another study, social capital was defined as a property of personal networks—the ability to reach others both inside and outside the organization for information, advice and problem solving (Burt 1992). As expected, both human capital and social capital had a positive effect on productivity. What was unexpected was the dominant effect of social capital—project managers with the best personal networks were most productive. They were better able to coordinate tasks and find the knowledge necessary to accomplish the goals of their projects.

Imagine if there was a way—for *free*, using the data and resources you already have—to design an organization where the individuals within it do the following:

- Are promoted sooner
- Close deals faster
- Receive larger bonuses
- Enhance team performance
- Reach team goals quicker
- Perform better as project managers
- Generate more creative solutions
- Increase research and development
- Coordinate projects more effectively
- Learn more about the firm's environment and marketplace
- Receive higher performance evaluations

Burt's research found ample empirical support for each of these workplace benefits of people with better social capital (1992).

As Michael Arena points out in his book *Adaptive Space*, traditional organizations rely on human capital strategies for innovation and growth, but adaptive space leans on social capital strategies (Arena 2018). Social capital can be thought of as the competitive advantage that is created based on the way an individual is connected to others. That is where adaptive space is created.

Human capital is what someone knows, while social capital is about how well someone is positioned to leverage what they know. Both are essential, yet organizations have dramatically overemphasized the former over the latter. According to Arena, organizations can scale innovation by facilitating connections, enabling information flow for "discovery, development, diffusion, and disruption" (Arena 2018). The first two, discovery and development, are represented by network positions, such as Hubs. Diffusion and disruption are most likely done by Gatekeepers and Pulsetakers. Ultimately, brokerage is key. The bridge connections between groups spark new ideas, and connections within the teams foster development of the ideas. These environments typically have high levels of trust, share information quickly, and increase the likelihood that ideas are accepted and applied.

Gatekeepers in the network can amplify ideas across the organization. Endorsement of new solutions into the formal operations system is often the biggest challenge, and it happens through network closure—the closing in around a potential sponsor of information flowing across multiple networks.

Classic attempts to share knowledge or implement a strategy have started with senior leadership who set "tone at the top" for the enterprise objectives. Using network science, we can show that this top-down, cascaded approach to spreading ideas will reach 20%–30% of an organization. However, if we identify the Hubs, Gatekeepers, and Pulsetakers in each network, we can reach and influence 80%–90% of the people in an organization. We can use these insights to create a movement.

Understanding these network dynamics gives anyone in the organization a powerful set of insights on why things happen the way they do—and more importantly, how to change the dynamics to serve the greater purpose of the organization. You can start to see how you can intentionally develop connections to weave together balanced networks and drive out bias and echoes that are not benefiting individuals, teams, or the organization at large.

How Networks Change

Networks react to what passes along their connections. With the spread of dangerous contagions, such as diseases or financial distress, people react with fear, cutting ties, isolating, and "turtling up." To get the picture, stop and think about the real tragedy of what happens when a turtle winds up rocking back and forth upside down on its shell. The problem is that the turtle thinks that everything is okay and has no idea that its demise is imminent.

This type of "turtled" network displays a propensity for higher clustering, strong tie interaction, and an intensification of insider versus outsider communication. But when there's important news, people may actively contact each other and increase a network's density—accelerating the spread of both good news and salacious rumors.

In *Social Networks Under Stress*, researchers Daniel Romero, Brian Uzzi, and Jon Kleinberg found that changes in network structure predict shifts in cognitive and affective processes (feelings and responses related to behaviors and beliefs) and the execution of new transactions. This shows the important predictive relationship between network structure and collective behavior within a social network. Small changes in connectedness can have enormous consequences (Romero, Uzzi, and Kleinberg 2016).

Even a change in the extent rather than the shape of our networks can have profound implications for contagion, immobility, and polarization (Jackson 2019). In organizational transformation, we see denser networks, more homophily, more polarization, and faster movement of information (Jackson 2019). As organization designers, we need to counteract the damaging side effects of homophily and improve the incentives to collect and spread accurate and deep information while learning to better filter the noise. Understanding the human network can increase connectivity and improve our collective intelligence and productivity instead of dividing society even more.

Know Your Networks

How is it, then, that we acquire network data? If you think back to the discussion on domain authority within the Google algorithm, you'll start to get a pretty good idea of how it's done.

Network data are now easily accessible. We can capture network insights using passive data that already exist in our organizations. Through the outputs of email, voicemail, and digital collaboration tools, such as Zoom, Teams, and Slack, we can create network maps and metrics that tell us exactly how our organization is working.

We can also use active data collection methods, such as short and simple surveys, that give us specific insights into the different types of work networks (knowledge, advice, innovation, etc.) and draw similar insights from the passive approach. Either method is effective, but combining them both provides the most powerful insights. The most important takeaway is that we now have communication tools and the ability to measure social patterns that are a better fit for our native desire for group efforts.

The relationships between people in an organization create the real pathways of knowledge. That's because the majority of the power of an organization exists in the structure of its network, not in the command-and-control hierarchy superimposed on it. Until very recently, we perceived organizations as vertical structures that were both blind and deaf to another life force within—the horizontal structure. Now, managers can anticipate how a decision they make will affect the informal organization by analyzing their network maps.

A great deal of interest is in how to create an innovative organization and, once an innovation has been developed, how to scale and spread the idea. Network design facilitates the connections necessary to provide a social bridge to transport ideas from entrepreneurial pockets found throughout the org into the more formal operational system (Arena 2018).

Tacit knowledge—the critical information that makes organizations functional—is, in fact, transferred through informal relationships, not through established channels within the formal hierarchy. This is particularly valuable when a company wants to anticipate reactions to change. For example, if a company wants to form a strategic team to remove key employees from the day-to-day operations of a division, they can design a map of the area without those players. If removing the central advice person from the network leaves the team with a group of isolated people, the manager should reconsider the strategy (Krackhardt and Hansen 1993).

Network patterns are a product of intentional behaviors rather than entrenched personality characteristics. In contrast to personality traits, behaviors can be taught or encouraged (Cross 2021). The relational space necessary for people to freely explore, exchange, and debate ideas can be intentionally architected. These designed networks enable an organization to positively disrupt themselves so they can control their own destiny before someone else does.

If you want your organization to learn something new, take a Gatekeeper in an innovation network and put them together with a Pulsetaker in an expert network, and you will get organizational learning. By putting people into different network roles, you can spread new ideas and get your good ones adopted by all. All this can be easily calculated and visualized—this is not so much art as science.

Let us draw from a paper published several years ago by organizational consultant and data scientist Valdis Krebs (2007). See the network picture in Figure 5.5. How could we improve the connectivity of these two teams?

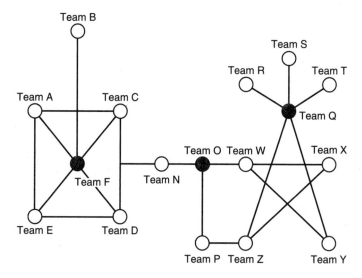

Figure 5.5   Network map of project teams.
Source: Krebs (2007) / Valdis Krebs

Better connections are those that provide you access to areas you currently do not have access to. Although Team F and Team Q each have many connections and have excellent local access (to the teams near them), they have only fair access to the rest of the network. Team O has the best social capital (i.e., network benefits) in this network of project teams. Team O achieves this with only three direct ties—it is connected to others who are well connected. Team O's indirect contacts bring access to information and knowledge not available locally. The average path length in this network is 3.45, with many paths longer than the network horizon. Even in this small network, some teams are nearly blind to what is happening in other parts of the network.

In the summer of 1998, writing in the scientific journal *Nature*, two Cornell mathematicians, Steven Strogatz and Duncan Watts, stirred excitement. While investigating small-world networks, they discovered that a few randomly added crosscuts between unconnected clusters would improve (i.e., lower) a network's characteristic path length significantly. The benefits were not just local, but spread throughout the network, and this improvement could be achieved with just a few added ties in the network. Very small adjustments could cause large positive changes—a common dynamic in complex adaptive systems (Krebs 2007).

Looking back on our project team network, how can we improve the connectivity with just one added link? Which two nodes would you connect to bring everyone in the network closer together? Although many combinations will increase the access of everyone to everyone else, the greatest measurable effect is when we add a crosscut between Team Q and Team F (see Figure 5.6). The average path length drops a whole step! The longest path in the network is reduced from seven steps to four steps. In human networks, the fewer steps in the network path, the quicker information arrives with less distortion.

The connection between Teams Q and F may be the optimal connection in network efficiency, but it may not be a practical connection. Both of these teams already have many ties and may not

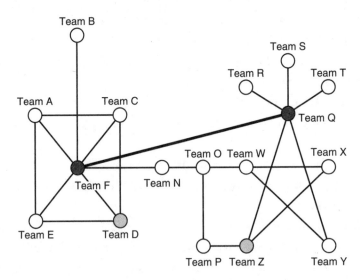

Figure 5.6   Adding a crosscut from Team F to Team Q.

Source: Krebs (2007) / Valdis Krebs

have the time and energy to support another. What is an alternative connection? If you cannot connect the highly connected nodes, how about connecting their respective network neighbors? Instead of connecting Q and F, how about connecting D and Z? This connection will not reduce the path length as much, but it is between nodes that are not overburdened with connections.

About That Story . . .

How did all of this work out regarding our hospital problem that opened this chapter? When we looked beyond organization charts, process maps, policy and procedure documents to also examine the networks within each of the hospitals, quite well, actually. Our analysis of networks opened doors that were not only closed but not even visible beforehand.

In the lowest performing hospital, the network picture showed us three critical takeaways. The first was that there were almost no core networks. Most of the individuals in this hospital were, at best, loosely connected in small groups. However, the second finding was that there was one exception. There was one dense core group in one department that was not connected to anyone else in the hospital. The third important finding was that a lot of individuals were isolated—very respected and experienced clinicians who, unfortunately, were on islands of their own.

What was once a total mystery to our client became obvious the moment she looked at the network maps! We quickly set about to address some of these fatal flaws. We increased the number of core networks by building teams around shared goals. We created new jobs and reporting relationships within the one department that had a dense core network to bridge between this department and others to spread ideas. Finally, we engaged the isolated individuals in specific roles that required them to engage with others who were connected in the network.

What did all of this mean in terms of a result? All of the hospitals in the group—those that were performing well and those that were not—were now connected. That led to the spread of good practices, more open communication, and more innovation. Within 12 months, the healthcare scorecard "triple aim" of better care, better health, and lower cost all showed positive improvements.

It didn't happen overnight, as this type of change takes time. After all, as they say, Rome wasn't built in a day. That said, after two years, the low-performing hospitals not only reached the level of the high-performing hospitals, but they even surpassed many of them. What was most important was that adverse events were curtailed and patients enjoyed better outcomes. This is what can happen when you replace failed vertical hierarchies with those that are more horizontal: It can literally save lives.

6

Hierarchy Versus Networks

"In matters of style, swim with the current; in matters of principle, stand like a rock."

—Thomas Jefferson

How well do the notions of hierarchy and networks coexist? A general tension exists between individual incentives to form relationships and what is best for society. If we all chose our relationships in order to improve communication and knowledge in our communities, we would engage with more people.

The two structures of hierarchy and networks exist in a dynamic interaction. By design, hierarchies are very slow to change. Hierarchies are great at dealing with small amounts of uncertainty. They consist of authorities, policy, rules and procedure formulation, and a goal of minimizing risk. And until now, this is the only structure we have ever focused on as organization designers.

With networks, you're really tracking the trust between people. Specifically, we're tracking the subtle calculations behind who is sought for knowledge, expertise, and innovation. Networks are relatively stable and can be slow to change without intervention.

59

Table 6.1   Formal hierarchy and informal networks.

Form	Hierarchy	Network
Work	Routine	Customized
Trust	Process	Reciprocity
Decisions	Defined	Delegated
Basis	Employment relationship	Complementary strengths
Context	Established	Ambiguous
Conflict resolution	Supervision	Reputation
Flexibility	Low/rigid	Medium/flexible
Relationship	Dependent/ transactional	Interdependent/trust
Visibility	Explicit	Tacit
Knowledge	Rules	Ropes
Diversity	Heterogeneity	Homogeneity
Discipline	Bilateral	Betrayal
Accountability	Transparent	Opaque
Rate of change	Slow, incremental	Rapid, radical

Source: Powell, 1990.

However, when risk or uncertainty arises, networks are "lighter on their feet" than hierarchies. When networks allocate resources, exchange occurs by individuals engaged in reciprocal, preferential, mutually supportive actions. Networks can be complex. The basic assumption of network relationships at work is that one party is dependent on resources controlled by another and that there are gains to be had by pooling resources. These relationships take considerable effort to establish and sustain (see Table 6.1).

At any one time, a network is stronger than a hierarchy. However, when measured over time, hierarchies are stronger than networks (Stephenson 2021). When you understand networks, you ultimately embrace that by assuming a particular position in the hierarchy, you may not be as connected as others will be in different reporting relationships.

This analysis is in no way an indictment of hierarchy. Hierarchy is an important aspect of an organization's structural integrity. That said, hierarchy's power cannot be confused with that of the equally real and relevant social networks that account for so much organizational knowledge. Hierarchy and networks should be yoked together to ensure balance and accountability (Stephenson 2021).

Working Together

The optimal relationship between these two structures is currently the subject of much research and debate. The key factor in how informal and formal structures influence an individual's performance is consistency. Consistency refers to the overlap between the vertical and horizontal networks.

For example, in a highly consistent organization, the formal authority lines mirror the informal social structure. A manager determines the responsibilities of supervisors, who then assign specific tasks to frontline workers. Even informally, the distribution of work does not change: Frontline workers depend on their supervisors for task assignments and guidance. This consistency prevents mixed or contradictory messages. Workers, for example, do not look for what they "really should be doing" from a person other than their supervisor.

Research shows that consistency between the formal authority network and informal networks led to better individual performance *to a point*. Ultimately, it depends on the sequential or reciprocal nature of the work (Soda and Zaheer 2012).

When considering the relationship between informal networks and the formal reciprocal workflow networks, the situation becomes much more complex. Workflow networks are the horizontal networks in the organization as opposed to the vertical authority networks.

Research has shown that greater inconsistency helps the individual perform at a higher level up to a certain point (Soda and Zaheer 2012). However, once past that point, even more inconsistency is too much for any situation, and the individual's performance starts to decline.

While more and more companies are recognizing the value of informal social networks, the challenge is to manage such networks for maximum effectiveness and efficiency. This highlights the error of believing that consistency—in other words, avoiding any diversity, contradictions, or incongruence between informal social networks and the company's formal structures and networks—is not necessarily the best course of action in all situations.

In situations that require employees and managers to make joint decisions and mutual adjustments, a trade-off must be carefully managed. On one hand, inconsistency can hurt performance because it reduces coordination. On the other, introducing different or complementary sources of information, ideas, and knowledge can improve performance.

Reciprocal workflows best suit cross-functional networks of teams. Hierarchies solve the need for orientation, structure, safety, direction, and reduction of complexity. Providing a simple hierarchical structure and a clear home base for people within their function and skill set is critical. In the home-base team, a leader cares for their development, well-being, and sense of belonging. In these teams, people meet their peers, exchange and develop their skills, or perform standard and repetitive operational work.

How to Change Existing Networks

When establishing the primary organizational characteristic, both the core capability and sequential nature of the work should be considered, as this is what should be placed in the hierarchy. (We will explore this further in Chapter 11: Purpose and Utility.) The reciprocal workflows best suit cross-functional networks of teams. Hierarchies solve the need for orientation, structure, safety, direction, and reduction of complexity. Providing a simple hierarchical structure and a clear home base for people within their function and skill set is critical. In the home-base team, a disciplinary leader cares for their development, well-being, and sense of belonging. In these home-base teams, people meet their peers, exchange and develop their skills, or perform standard and repetitive operational work.

Building Distributed Networks

Even though silos do cause all the problems that we attribute to them—including wasted time, increased friction, ineffective communications, untimely decision-making, unresponsiveness, and loss of business—they're simply not going to go away just because we complain about them. The only way we can effectively get rid of them is if we can replace the entire system on which they're built (King 2020). Now that we have the ability to make the invisible visible through network analytics and can compare these horizontal relationships to that of hierarchy, we are finally in a position to connect the silos that stop our organizations from being effective.

Building distributed networks is the answer to intentionally connecting dysfunctional silos. What happens when silos lead to dysfunction within an organization? When business leaders are overly controlling and protective of their resources, they risk endangering their companies. Changing our management paradigm from accumulation and control to movement and sharing can reverse that trend.

In design terms, the research indicates that organizations should make efforts to intentionally create networks. This can be done by organizing forums, designing office spaces that are conducive to informal interactions, or creating inter-functional teams. Other intervention techniques include the following:

- Job rotation: Employees get to experience life in different parts of the organization.
- Temporary work groups: Employees carry out isolated tasks separate from their day jobs in new groups (e.g., quality circles).
- Permanent work groups: Employees carry out tasks separate from their day jobs in new groups.
- Informal meetings: Managers organize informal meetings to share information and build relationships.
- Performance objectives and incentives: Objectives and incentives focus on driving intentional collaboration and outcomes, not just personal goals.

- Communities of practice: Employees informally share information around particular practices that are important to the organization.

At the same time, there is no need, as perhaps previously thought, to ensure a perfect fit between formal and informal networks in all situations. As any good consultant will tell you, "it depends." The good news is we now know what good looks like for the informal networks. Whether your business objective is growth, innovation, scaling best practices, or efficient and consistent service delivery, we can identify the network patterns needed and intentionally create those patterns.

7

Measurement

"People with targets and jobs dependent upon meeting them will probably meet the targets even if they have to destroy the enterprise to do it."

—W. Edwards Deming, *The New Economics for Industry, Government, Education* (1993)

At a Fortune 500 company, our point of contact was one of a few business unit presidents with the organization. What that really meant was that, in the eyes of the rest of the organization and his superiors in particular, he was responsible for a multibillion-dollar profit-and-loss (P&L) statement. Our mission at that moment was to convince him that we needed to get more enterprise services embedded into his business and figure out how we could repurpose some key resources in his business unit to participate in cross-functional, agile teams that served all the business unit presidents.

Needless to say, he was far from excited about that concept. To be blunt, he was downright grumpy.

"Why should I give you any of my people for this effort?" he asked sullenly. "When our CEO looks at my performance, he only looks at my P&L results, not how well we played in the sandbox with the rest of the businesses. And let's not forget 60% of my salary is based on achieving my businesses' profitability targets." *This amount, as you can imagine, was not insignificant.* "Whatever you are trying to do here better not jeopardize my bonus."

Sadly, he was not wrong. Despite everyone agreeing that working in a more integrated fashion was the only way the enterprise would win in the market, the metrics in place incentivized siloed, territorial behaviors.

What was happening here—and what happens far too often across the professional landscape in society—is that people are, rightly, hung up on their own evaluations and the metrics contained therein. The problem with that thinking is that the specifics of these evaluations are often at odds with what would transform an organization in a positive manner.

This executive *knew* that our ideas would help the organization, but he also *knew,* rightly, that agreeing to this approach would possibly harm his own metrics and, as a result, his personal pocketbook. It's a conundrum that persists and exists in every industry. Why put on an enterprise hat when you already have your own hat that you get well-paid to wear?

Is Performance Measurement Necessary?

It has been said that if strategy is the blueprint for an organization, metrics are the concrete, wood, and drywall. Yet every day, at almost every company, strategy is being hijacked by numbers (Harris and Tayler 2019). For an extreme example of this, look to Wells Fargo, where employees opened 3.5 million deposit and credit card accounts without customers' consent in an effort to implement its now-infamous "cross-selling" strategy (Harris and Tayler 2019).

Closer examination suggests that Wells Fargo never actually had a cross-selling strategy; it had a cross-selling metric. In its third-quarter 2016 earnings report, the bank mentions an effort to "best align our cross-sell metric with our strategic focus on long-term retail banking relationships." In other words, Wells Fargo had—and still has—a strategy of building long-term customer relationships, and management intended to track the degree to which it was accomplishing that goal by measuring cross-selling. In a case of truly brutal irony, a focus on the metric unraveled many of the bank's valuable long-term relationships (Harris and Tayler 2019).

One of management consulting's most influential thinkers, Peter Drucker, believed that if you can't measure it, you can't improve it. At a basic level, adding a business's revenue sources and subtracting from that all the business's expenses to get a sense of how profitable a revenue stream is seems pretty important to staying in business.

But systems, like magical wishes in fairy tales, have a terrible tendency to produce exactly and only what you ask them to produce, so be careful what you ask for in this regard. For example, if the desired system state is good education, measuring that goal by the amount of money spent per student will ensure money is spent per student. If the quality of education is measured by performance on standardized tests, the system will produce better performance on standardized tests. Whether either of these measures is correlated with good education is far from settled.

Steven Kerr's famous article "On the Folly of Rewarding A, While Hoping for B" makes the point that rewards must be aligned with organizational goals and desired behaviors; if they're not, the desired outcomes are not likely to manifest (in fact, the opposite may occur) (Kerr 1995). Kerr provides several examples of misaligned incentives to highlight his point.

One example focuses on teamwork. Coaches of most sports prefer to speak of teamwork and diminish focus on individual accomplishments. But when you think about it, rewards in sports are usually distributed according to individual performance. For example, the college basketball player who passes to his teammates instead of shooting will have lower scoring statistics and, therefore, is less likely to be drafted. Thus, it is rational for players to think of themselves first and the team second.

All types of measures can be tied to individual goals, department targets, and, ultimately, the compensation of individuals and the financial success of the organization. On its face, setting goals and targets and measuring progress toward these targets seems logical and even motivating. Realistically, it is unlikely that measurement can or should be removed from organizational life. That said, the behavioral impacts of budgets, goals, and targets, and the act of tying these things to compensation, must be understood and addressed in our architecture.

Performance Reviews

Is there anything more universally despised by leaders and team members alike than performance reviews? The truth is that people need attention, and when you give it to them in a safe and nonjudgmental environment, they stay, and they work.

Yes, feedback is attention, and research shows even negative feedback has some positive impact over no feedback. However, negative feedback doesn't enable learning. In fact it *inhibits* learning. Positive attention, meanwhile, is 30 times more powerful than negative attention in creating high performance (Kerr 1995).

Stop rating performance. Not only do the ratings have negative consequences on performance, but we all know that managers and their teams loathe them. In the real world, none of the methods, meetings, or carefully calibrated rating scales works. This is because all of them are based on the belief that people can reliably rate other people. They can't, as copious research shows.

Think about a forced ranking performance evaluation system that requires leaders to identify at least half of their employees as below average. Yet ample research consistently shows team performance matches a power law distribution more than a bell curve (O'Boyle and Aguinis 2012). We have known this for decades, yet most organizations still force rankings on a curve!

Everyone displays their own rating pattern. The rating you get tells you more about the rating pattern of your manager than about your performance (Buckingham and Goodall 2019). Opponents of ratings cite the cognitive biases inherent in them, particularly anchoring and halo effects, as well as the immense organizational time commitment needed to review, rate, and calibrate.

We lived through this problem in one of my former companies. During the performance review process, each manager had exactly 3 minutes to "tell the employee's story" regarding their performance for the previous year. Managers who had better reputations were given less scrutiny, and leaders asked fewer questions about their team members. So in reality, the employee's performance was not judged; instead, it was the effectiveness of the manager's presentation. While it was up to the managers to provide completely unbiased views and dispassionate perspectives, they could actually personally benefit from showing off their own skills and testing their political capital. Savvy employees would try to get on certain managers' teams, knowing they would have a better performance review and thus better compensation increases. No wonder some managers were more popular than others!

Give Attention

Dan Ariely, researcher and author, experimented with the idea of the fruits of our labor. He took a sheet of paper with random letters on it and asked subjects to find pairs of letters. He paid them a small amount of money to complete the sheet. Then he asked if they would like to do another sheet for a little less money. If so, he repeated the process, only for even less money. He continued this approach until at some point the subject decided to stop, realizing that continuing was not worth the effort (Ariely 2013).

Three conditions were present in this experiment. In the first condition, people wrote their name on the sheet, found all the pairs of letters, and gave the sheet to the experimenter. The experimenter then scanned the paper, said, "Uh huh," and put it on a pile of papers on their desk. In the second condition, people did not write their name on the piece of paper. The experimenter didn't look at it either. It was simply placed on a pile. In the third condition, the experimenter did not look at the paper. Instead, it was placed directly into the shredder.

What happened? In the acknowledged conditions, the first situation previously described, people worked all the way down to 15 cents before stopping. When the experimenter simply placed the paper into the shredder, subjects worked half as much. What about the ignored condition? As it turns out, it was almost like the shredder.

Ignoring people's performance is almost as bad as shredding their efforts before their eyes. The mere act of looking at work doubles people's motivation (Ariely 2013). The good news is you can dramatically improve motivating conditions simply by acknowledging someone's work. When that doesn't happen, or even when organizations move toward the other end of the spectrum, it can damage overall worker morale and individual and collective fulfillment.

Traditional performance management is a highly detested construct, even among those conducting evaluations. Who finds value in plowing through annual paperwork, making a quick decision on the things someone did wrong some time ago that they no longer have the opportunity to correct, followed by writing lofty goal-setting documents that are never glanced at again?

Today's focus is on gaining skills, experience, and feedback on an ongoing basis to improve an individual's ability to perform the tasks in their role and potentially expand or change roles based on these improvements. Looking back—especially in secret—does not accomplish any of these goals. Real-time, in-the-moment feedback, delivered with good intention and as transparently as possible, corrects and/or bolsters behavior exponentially more than a five-paragraph essay delivered 6 months after the fact.

System Measurements: Profit and Loss

To further this understanding, let's look at the most common system measurement—profit and loss—how it works today and how it can be improved. Next, let's examine the measures we use today to assess and reward individual performance—namely goals, the rating of individual performance assessment against these goals, and the corresponding incentives and rewards provided to the individual. For each of these, let's understand what is problematic today, why it's driving the wrong behaviors, and what to do about it.

Assigning P&L accountability to a general manager is a common means of establishing clear ownership for a capability area, be it function, product, service, geography, or customer segment. Business leaders naturally want their scope of authority to match their assigned accountability, and many top executives, including CEOs, are drawn to these models of accountability. In fact, many consider a sign of a mature, high-potential leader as one who has managed a P&L.

Unfortunately, this often leads to simplistic overuse of fully loaded, heavyweight function, division, or customer teams that operate independently, when in fact they should be leveraging more of the assets of the enterprise. This is not recommended (Morieux and Tollman 2014)! This mismatch creates the perception of accountability, but not only do these organizations have higher cost structures with a great deal of duplication and unrewarded complexity, very often they conflict with the need for more boundary-spanning ways of working (Kates, Kesler, and DiMartino 2021). Companies that make their P&L the cornerstone of accountability end up with multiple P&Ls—per region, business unit, key customer account, products, etc.

Another critical factor to P&L is control over resources. We like to talk about key resources as our companies' lifeblood, the most important thing we need to survive or to be successful, and yet we pay no attention to their movement between different parts of an organization. Blood by itself does not ensure life. It's the movement, the flow of the blood that counts.

Our lives depend on flows of nutrients both inside our bodies, enabled by the circulatory system, and between our bodies and the outside world, achieved through the continuous act of breathing. Embolisms and other blockages that stop those flows cause death to tissue, limbs, organs, or even to the whole organism (King 2020).

If our bodies decided to try out our corporate model of resource management, and our hearts started to store blood instead of pumping it to where it is needed and our lungs started to hold their breath instead of continually bringing in fresh resources from the outside and sharing them with the blood, we would die immediately. To exist, living organisms use pumps (lines of business), a circulatory system (hierarchy, networks, and measurement), and enriching environments (membership, teaming, and responsibility).

The value-destroying effects of poorly aligned metrics that organization design consultants Amy Kates, Greg Kesler, and Michelle DiMartino describe include individual performance targets competing with business goals to the detriment of the business overall (King 2020). This leads to rational decisions being made to optimize performance in one unit to hurt the enterprise.

Most organizations have not changed their measurement system to align and reinforce their organization design, thereby creating friction, slow decision-making, duplication, and unrewarded complexity. No amount of "enterprise mindset" or "collaborative skill building" will overcome this fundamental issue: *The context that has been designed and the behaviors that are desired are in conflict.*

Collaborative P&L

Establishing collaborative P&Ls is one way to address the negative impacts of separate P&L. In the collaborative P&L that Kates, Kesler and DiMartino describe in *Networked, Scaled, and Agile* (2021), there are two complementary sets of financial and customer metrics. Let's say, in this example, products are the primary organizing characteristic and geography is the secondary. (These concepts will be further explored in Chapter 11: Purpose and Utility.) Profit-and-loss targets will be composed of some metrics that are shared by the global business team and the regional sales and service team. The shared metrics are identical for each of the partners.

Top-line revenue targets for product sales will be shared, a revenue target is owned by leaders in specific regions or countries, and those results will roll up worldwide to be owned by someone in a global product-management position (Kates, Kesler, and DiMartino 2021). In this context, revenue is a shared metric, but other targets will be unique to one of the other roles, focused more on line-of-sight. These controllable metrics are results that one partner will have more impact on because of the nature of their role.

There is a balance to be achieved in the way these metrics are set between line-of-sight and collaborative approaches. The most important aspect of finding this artful balance is to avoid directly competing P&L metrics that disrupt cross-group agreements (Kates, Kesler, and DiMartino 2021). The other critical aspect is the linkage of these system-level measures to individual and team goals, feedback, and rewards. Taken together, aligned metrics and rewards ultimately drive greater shareholder value.

To take a well-cited example, when Steve Jobs arrived back at Apple to resume his position as chief executive officer (CEO), Apple had a conventional structure for a company of its size and scope. It was divided into business units, each with its own P&L responsibilities. As is often the case with decentralized business units, managers were inclined to fight with one another. Believing that conventional management had stifled innovation, Jobs, in his first year returning as CEO, laid off the general managers of all the business units (in a single day), put the entire company under one P&L, and combined the disparate functional departments of the business units into one functional organization (Podolny and Hansen 2020).

Remarkably, Apple retains this structure today, even though the company is nearly 40 times as large in terms of revenue and far more complex than it was in 1998. The bonuses of senior R&D executives are based on company-wide performance numbers rather than the costs of or revenue from particular products. The CEO occupies the only position on the organizational chart where the design, engineering, operations, marketing, and retail of any of Apple's main products meet.

In effect, besides the CEO, the company operates with no conventional general managers: people who control an entire process from product development through sales and are judged according to a P&L statement (Podolny and Hansen 2020).

Individual Goals Versus Shared Goals

We know we need some measurement in order to stay in business, but we also know we need to be very careful of the unintended consequences of goals that work at cross-purposes in our organizations. In *Nine Lies About Work*, well-known business consultants and leadership experts Marcus Buckingham and Ashley Goodall say, "Goals set by others imprison us." They believe this because "pressure to achieve company-imposed goals is coercion, and coercion is a cousin to fear. . . . Sales goals don't beget more sales; they just anticipate what the sales will be. Sales goals are for performance prediction, not performance creation" (Buckingham and Goodall 2019).

Professor of organizational behavior Dan Cable shows us in *Alive at Work* what can happen if you tie these goals to individual rewards (Cable 2019). Consider the following: When lab technicians put two young rats together, they almost always start to play—pouncing, chasing, and wrestling each other. We know it's play because of the rats' laughter (Cable 2019). (Yes, rats laugh!) Just like humans, rat play is a form of learning and experimenting. The researchers measured the rats' laughter and playfulness before they put a small tuft of cat fur in their play space. The smell of the fur activated the rats' innate fear system. Play dropped to zero. What they were seeing was the inhibiting relationship between the seeking system and the fear system.

The concept of the negativity bias has become quite well-known in recent years. Our brains evolved for survival so that negative emotions dominate positive emotions. Losing money, being abandoned by friends or colleagues in your networks, and receiving criticism all have a greater impact on people than winning money, gaining friends, and receiving praise.

Now consider our metrics in large companies—individual goals and metrics—which are tied to performance, feedback, and ultimately pay and promotion. All these policies that make us anxious about losing pay, promotions, and status are exactly like the cat fur in that our fear system shuts off our seeking system. This is a biological inhibition of our creativity.

The frame of performance management and pay for performance leaves our seeking system very little chance (Cable 2019). We have created a system at work that kills our human nature to be curious, to experiment, to innovate, and to be happy.

Yet despite scientific proof that our goal-setting practices don't work, Buckingham and Goodall point out that one Big Four firm spends $450 million a year on setting, tracking, and evaluating goals every year, and another major consulting firm spends double that. "When companies like these shell out close to $1 billion on something every year, there must be some truly extraordinary results" (Buckingham and Goodall 2019).

As it happens, no research exists that shows goals set for you from above stimulate you to greater productivity. As Buckingham and Goodall note, "Goals are about stimulating the performance of your people in the right direction. The problem is, in the real world there is stuff to be done. Work is work; goals are not" (2019). Instead, evidence shows that cascaded goals actually limit performance (Buckingham and Goodall 2019). But goals can be good; they just need to be set voluntarily and be focused on learning. Simply put, learning goals are more effective at improving performance in a changing environment where innovation is important. This is because they draw our attention away from the end result and encourage us instead to use curiosity to discover novel strategies.

Shared goals are naturally developed over time through social interaction and experience (Clarridge 2020). People can reach shared goals when they can understand each other's perspectives, common difficulties, and opportunities for mutual benefit. They are developed from a sense of shared identity and togetherness and from shared experiences. When individuals identify with a group, their concern for collective processes and outcomes is enhanced, which increases the chances that collaboration will occur (Clarridge 2020).

Shared goals, set by teams themselves, are a cornerstone of the agile methodology. At a high level, agile can be defined as a results-focused approach to designing and implementing products or services that has its origins in software development. The approach organizes autonomous "scrum" teams who engage in continuous prioritization/reprioritization of their workflows to get minimum viable products to market. The teams are asked to develop their own team goals as an essential part of the methodology. But all too often, these are cited as the most difficult things to implement, and why many agile transformations are not successful. Organizations are typically unwilling to accept teams setting their own goals or accept team goals over individual ones.

But if an organization sees the value in shared goals, various activities can help with their development, such as jointly developing plans, budgets, procedures, rules, roles, and agreements that participants believe will achieve the desired outcomes. When people are empowered by these activities, they tend to develop commitment and trust, both contributing to an increase in social capital (Clarridge 2020).

People tend to be reinforced by success and diminished by unmet expectations, failure, and a lack of clarity. When a group achieves or makes progress toward shared goals, the belief in the goals tends to strengthen. Setting achievable goals can help to quickly reinforce a sense of common purpose, solidarity, and trust. This effect can be magnified by acknowledging and celebrating the achievement of, or progress toward, shared goals. The attitudes toward shared goals are reinforced by the narrative, which is powerfully shaped by influential actors' reactions to events and outcomes.

Rewards Linked to Motivation

The basic strategy we use for raising children, teaching students, and managing workers can be summarized in six words: Do *this,* and you'll get *that.* We dangle goodies (from candy bars to sales commissions) in front of people in much the same way we train the family pet. Drawing on a wealth of psychological research, Alfie Kohn points the way to a more successful strategy based on working with people instead of doing things to them. "Do rewards motivate people?" Kohn asks. "Yes. They motivate people to get rewards" (2018).

We recently worked with a software company, and as part of its organization transformation, we had the leaders describe their job in one sentence as though they were speaking to a child. The Total Rewards leader in the human resource function described their role as "the ability to deliver treats for a job well done." Although the administration of incentives can be straightforward to highly complex, almost all companies remain almost solely focused on extrinsic rewards as the primary motivator.

In *Drive: The Surprising Truth About What Motivates Us,* Daniel Pink (2011) summarizes a rich body of evidence based on many decades of psychology research that intrinsic motivation is often supported by three key factors: autonomy, mastery, and purpose. High effort and performance often result from designing jobs to provide freedom of choice, the chance to develop one's skills and expertise, and the opportunity to do work that matters. Evidence also supports the importance of a fourth factor: a sense of connection with other people.

Our brains have a seeking system that creates the natural impulse to explore our world, learn, and extract meaning. When we follow the urges of our seeking system, it releases dopamine, a neurotransmitter linked to motivation and pleasure. The seeking system is a neural network that runs between the prefrontal cortex and the ventral striatum. These circuits appear to be major contributors to our feeling of engagement and excitement (Cable 2019). Said another way, we are all born with a growth mindset. In *Alive at Work*, Daniel M. Cable (2019) examines the neuroscience underlying these theories of motivation. He shows us that we are motivated to do a lot of things based on hope and aspiration that are not described by backward-looking rewards. In other words, you cannot motivate people, but you can demotivate them! Why is this?

Paying for performance robs you of your control and autonomy and, therefore, motivation. It also diminishes performance and stifles creativity. Pink (2011) cites a summary of 51 studies on pay for performance, showing researchers concluded that paying for performance has a negative influence on performance. Yet despite the overwhelming evidence, our human resource practices are built entirely on carrots and sticks—a mechanistic reward and punishment approach that often does not work and actually inflicts harm on individuals and organizations as a whole.

First published more than 35 years ago, cheekily titled *Up the Organization*, former Avis Rent-a-Car President Robert Townsend famously wrote, "You cannot motivate people. That door is locked from the inside" (Townsend and Bennis 2007). People are intrinsically motivated. You cannot motivate, but you can demotivate. Despite having these insights at our fingertips for more than 50 years, our business and human resources policies do not take advantage of our understanding of human motivation. The good news is you can create the context for motivation to show up (Townsend and Bennis 2007).

Transform Individual Rewards

If we want to architect our measurement systems for more engaged workers, we need to avoid doing more of the wrong things, like investing in sweeter carrots or sharper sticks (Townsend and Bennis 2007). We desire to do things because they matter, they are interesting, they are part of something important, or for some inherent and internal reason. This is not just for millennials or Gen Z; this applies to workers born in all decades. We are motivated by autonomy to direct our own lives, by the desire to get better at something that matters, and by purpose or a yearning to do what we do in service of something larger than ourselves. If twentieth-century management was about compliance, architecting rewards for the twenty-first century means paying fairly and getting money *off* the table (Townsend and Bennis 2007).

Many organizations have begun to adopt alternative approaches to determine pay, some of which have even resulted in higher employee engagement and productivity. These approaches include equal bonus outcomes for all, a differentiated bonus approach, manager discretion and market rate—all of which continue to remain the top trends of managing pay without ratings. At W. L. Gore & Associates, where most of the company is employee owned, compensation is decided by a panel of peers.

The purpose of rewards is, after all, to increase performance. Human nature shows that the closer a reward is to a behavior, the greater the influence the reward has on increasing that behavior. So, instead of waiting for an annual review, companies can choose to reward top performers in real time. Some companies are shifting to more frequent compensation discussions and allowing managers to distribute bonuses on an ongoing basis.

Collective Incentives

Findings show that companies with collaborative goals outperform the market 5.5 times (Townsend and Bennis 2007)! For an example of equal bonus outcomes for all, Motorola disbanded its annual four-point rating scale. Compensation was decoupled from performance. Standard bonuses are now paid as a percentage of an employee's salary, determined solely on company performance, with an additional pool of 25% set aside to reward top performers in real time.

Despite the evidence that high-performance organizations are emphasizing collaboration in performance goals, it seems that most companies are not taking advantage of this idea. In Pink's research, only about 25% of the organizations studied align effective collaboration with their employee performance management processes. And in Deloitte's 2020 Human Capital Trends Report, only 37% of companies consider team-based rewards in their compensation strategy (Schwartz et al. 2020).

Shared goals attach meaning to performance, which makes it easier to evaluate individual and group actions and encourage change where required. Shared goals are a powerful motivator for collective action.

Global leadership professor Rob Cross says, "When we look at networks within companies, 3 to 5% of people account for 20 to 35% of the value-added ties, yet if we compare our lists of who these critical people are against who the company is paying attention to—who is getting the biggest bonuses or in the top talent programs—there's typically only a 50% overlap. What we're learning is that by applying more of a collaborative focus around what creates high performers, we can figure out how to manage talent differently in a much finer tuned way" (Schwartz et al. 2020).

So, what of the grumpy president I mentioned earlier? The one who was laser-focused on meeting his businesses revenue and profit targets, regardless of the impact of this pursuit to the larger enterprise? While I cannot attest to his enduring cheerfulness, I can say with confidence we made some strides in aligning the measurement of the business to the desired enterprise teaming behaviors. First, we recommended a revision to the P&L structure across all the businesses. While we did not change the primary organizing characteristic of the business units (BUs), we did put in place shared revenue and profitability goals and matched this system structure to individual incentives, so that all the market-facing C-suite roles had skin in the game.

With these new collaborative measures and rewards in place at the top, this executive and his peers were motivated to share resources to work horizontally across all the BUs. We set up new teams that had shared goals and corresponding incentives based on delivering enterprise results that were not subservient to any one business unit's targets. Today, these teams have expanded and are acknowledged in the media and by shareholders as critical components to realizing enterprise goals. They also have exceeded their shared profitability goals, and the overall revenue for the company has increased.

Not a bad return for simply recasting internal targets!

8

Membership

"People are taking personal issues that are not personal. They go with the territory. And once you deeply understand the territory, you can change the experience."

—Barry Oshray, *Context, Context, Context* (2018)

The critical importance of identifying as a member in a group became clear to me one day when I was flying cross-country on a major commercial airline that had gone through a bumpy merger with another large airline the year before. I had the fortune of being upgraded to business class, but the misfortune of sitting in the bulkhead aisle seat, which affords a comfortable seat and some food, but little privacy or peace because it is the central hub for the flight attendants. As such, I could not help but notice that there was quite a disagreement going on between two of the flight attendants. "Disagreement" may be putting it too kindly. Between the swearing under their breath, the slamming of cups and glasses in the galley, and the obvious daggers that were shooting out of their eyes, I couldn't help but notice something was seriously adrift.

About halfway through the flight, it became apparent to us bulkhead passengers that these two employees were from different legacy organizations. These legacy companies had been known for different corporate cultures, and one side had fared better than the other during the integration. At around this time, a third attendant entered the picture and innocently shed light on the fact that, actually, they were both from the *same* legacy organization, but they had not known one another before.

This changed the entire dynamic immediately and totally. Within a second, they went from plotting to throw one another out the plane door to braiding each other's hair. There was no leadership change, team-building exercise, or trust fall. Simply the realization that they were from the same group led to a complete transformation in their behavior toward one another and, frankly, toward us passengers.

Why? How? Is there an explanation for such a remarkable transformation?

We know from our discussion of homophily that being separate can stimulate differentiation and enable our differences to grow. Conversely, integration produces feelings of belonging. The pattern of an organization, which consists of all the networks, including the hierarchy network, has predictable consequences for how we experience and relate to one another.

There is something both troubling and exciting in understanding this—that our impressions of one another are not as unchangeable as we may believe. In *Context, Context, Context*, Oshray (2018) sums it up: "I feel the way I feel about you or your group not because of who you are but because we are apart, and if we integrated in some meaningful way I would feel very different about you or your group."

At work we are typically members of a functional silo with clear roles and reporting, and then we participate on multiple cross-functional teams with unique supervisors, roles, and responsibilities. Because we are all members of one or more groups at work, we are typically at best competing and at worst operating at cross-purposes. To create a sense of belonging, we must thoughtfully structure our groups and thus stop creating patterns that create frustration and disengagement.

In-Group and Out-Group

The academic literature is rich and consistent in explaining how deeply rooted these tendencies are in our species. Social identity theory explains intergroup behavior in relation to the discrimination of in-group members (us) against out-group members (them). Social identity is a person's sense of who they are based on their group membership(s). In 1979, social psychologist Henri Tajfel proposed a now widely accepted theory that stereotyping (i.e., putting people into groups and categories) is based on a normal cognitive process: the tendency to group things together (Islam 2014). In doing so, we tend to exaggerate the differences between groups and the similarities of things in the same group. The central hypothesis of social identity theory is that group members of an in-group will seek to find negative aspects of an out-group, thus enhancing their own self-image.

Further additions to the field support the deep and enduring tendencies for us versus them. Social categorization theory emphasizes the individual tendency to categorize into groups that share a series of values and interpretations (Edmondson and Harvey 2017). Similarity-attraction theory is another explanation that posits that people like and are attracted to those who are similar, rather than dissimilar, to themselves.

Numerous empirical studies drawn from these theories have shown that unclear social identity *or multiple social identities* are detrimental to team cohesion. This is a critical point given the multiple roles we are asked to play at work each day, often with unique and even conflicting identities.

Now, we know from our review of networks in Chapter 5 that relationships that lead to feelings of membership don't form at random. Specific conditions contribute to the depth and speed at which they form. These can be categorized in the following two ways:

1. Similarity within and competition between, specifically:
   - Frequent, repeated interaction with a new group of people
   - A high degree of overlap between relationships in the new group
   - A high *density* of people in network proximity
   - Other groups that are perceived as competition
2. A shared sense of fate, specifically:
   - Going through something difficult and perhaps fear-inducing together
   - Unifying goals
   - A transition period where people are open to changing or evolving their identity

When we apply these concepts to organizational life, it is easy to see that the frequent connections to functions, departments, or geographies in which we work drive our sense of membership. This is further solidified by sharing goals that are lined up to these functions or departments and having individual rewards largely based on these functions or departments reaching their goals. Let's take a deeper look.

Affinity Within Groups Is Amplified by Similarity Within and Competition Between

Let's start with the loyalty/betrayal foundation, which is perhaps best characterized by one of the most famous studies in social psychology, that of the Rattlers and the Eagles by social psychologist Muzafer Sherif.

In 1954, Sherif conducted a study where he brought two groups of 12-year-old boys to summer camp on separate consecutive days, basing them in different parts of the camp, so that each group thought they were alone (Sherif 1988).

Norms, songs, rituals, and distinctive identities began to form in each group. For example, the Rattlers were tough and never cried, while Eagles never cursed. On day six of the experiment, Sherif let the Rattlers get close enough to the baseball field to hear that the other boys, the Eagles, were using it, even though the Rattlers had claimed it as their field. The Rattlers begged the camp counselors to let them challenge the Eagles to a baseball game.

As planned from the start, Sherif arranged a weeklong tournament of sports competitions and camping skills. From that point forward, Sherif said all activities became competitive. Tent pitching, baseball, and other activities were undertaken with more zest and also with more efficiency.

Tribal behavior increased dramatically. Both sides created flags and hung them in contested territory. They raided and vandalized each other's bunks, called each other nasty names, and would have come to blows without the camp counselors' interventions. Sherif remarked that anyone who came in at this point would have concluded that these youngsters were wicked and vicious. Yet, of course, it was group processes rather than personality that had produced the conflict (Sherif 1988).

The role of groups in human evolution is perhaps the most important driver of behavior in organizations today. We evolved with an inherent set of tribal instincts. We love to mark group membership, and then we cooperate preferentially with members of our group.

In hunter-gatherer times, people lived in much denser webs of norms, subjecting each other to informal sanctions and occasionally violent punishments. Those who could navigate skillfully and maintain good reputations were rewarded by gaining the trust, cooperation, and political support needed to obtain progressively more influence (Sherif 1988).

What made us evolutionarily fit was a remarkable kind of friendliness, a virtuosic ability to coordinate and communicate with others that allowed us to achieve all the cultural and technical marvels in human history. In *Survival of the Friendliest*, the authors state that this gift for friendliness comes at a cost (Hare and Woods 2020). Just as a mother bear is most dangerous around her cubs, we are at our most dangerous when someone we love is threatened by an outsider. The threatening outsider is demoted to subhuman, which makes this person fair game for our worst instincts. Cognitive evolution reveals that the same traits that make us the most tolerant species on the planet also make us the cruelest.

People form bonds of trust with other people like them. In *Humankind*, Dutch historian Rutger Bregman (2020) writes, "Contact engenders more trust, more solidarity, and more mutual kindness. It helps you see the world through other people's eyes." This sounds a lot like when Abraham Lincoln famously said, "I don't like that man. I must get to know him better." These examples illustrate the principle of propinquity, which in many ways is similar to proximity. This is the reason you marry the girl next door, a concept that is best described as "familiarity breeds liking." The mere-exposure effect is a psychological phenomenon by which people tend to develop a preference for things merely because they are familiar with them. In studies of interpersonal attraction, the more often someone sees a person, the more pleasing and likeable they find that person.

I have seen this play out time and again in organizations. During a recent reorganization project, two of the executives we worked with seemed diametrically opposed in every way, personally and professionally; however, as a result of restructuring, they became leaders of two parts of the same function. Seeing this, the suggestion by their chief executive officer (CEO) was simple enough: a standing weekly meeting followed by a mandatory lunch together. From initial grumbling, a loose camaraderie formed. What started with, "Can you believe the CEO is making us do this?" became information sharing, grudging respect, and then open communication and collaboration. The time together became familiar and not unwelcome. And now, friendly with one another, they have continued to protect this time together as the information sharing and trust have proved to be valuable for them as individuals.

Affinity Within Groups Is Amplified by a Shared Sense of Fate

Given our discussion on misaligned goals and incentives from Chapter 7: Measurement, I should not be continually surprised by how polarizing our workplaces are today. And you only have to look at politics today in the United States to see a replication of the tension I see in companies. In the US political landscape, friendships and social contacts among elected officials across party lines became discouraged in the 1990s. Once the human connections were weakened, it became easier to treat members of the other party as the permanent enemy rather than fellow members of an elite club. As one elder congressman put it, "This is not a collegial body anymore. . . . Members walk into the chamber full of hatred" (Haidt 2012).

Social psychologist Jonathan Haidt suggests that in the United States we are losing our competitive edge relative to the rest of the world because of the disunity between conservative and liberal groups. This dynamic occurs in a similar fashion, albeit at a smaller scale, within large organizations (Haidt 2012). To combat this, we must find meaningful ways to create intentional connections between our defined groups in organizations.

Shared goals and shared purpose are commonly mentioned as elements of social capital. They are the collective aspirations of actors and the sense of shared destiny with others (Adler and Kwon 2002). Shared goals are a force that holds people together and allows actors to coordinate their efforts and work together for mutual benefit (Chow and Chan 2008). Shared goals are more than just established and documented goals. They are the shared belief that a person's interests are represented by the group and that working for the benefit of the group will progress personal interests now or in the future. Shared goals exist when people believe that their actions will be appropriately reciprocated by others and they will meet their obligations and expectations (Lesser and Prusak 1999). As such, it is strongly associated with belonging, solidarity, and trust.

The intensity that a shared sense of fate has on human behavior can be explained using evolutionary psychology. Haidt describes the evolution of reputation, reciprocity, and suppression of free riders. Evolving into big-brained *Homo sapiens* demanded extensive cooperation, so we are hardwired to be social, work in groups, and consider what is best for the collective. When people have a sense of shared fate, it really brings out the cooperative nature in us. As a result, in any organization, it is important to suppress free riders because they are poisonous. To discourage such behavior, it is important to harness reputational concerns as much as possible to get good cooperate outcomes.

In *Humankind,* Bregman (2020) suggests that our innate eagerness to please and to be liked—and, crucially, our ability to feel shame—are driving forces in our advancement on both individual and collective levels. Said another way, we are obsessively concerned about what others think of us. We come by this groupishness through evolutionary means, which is why it is so incredibly quick to take place and so hard to undo.

Charles Darwin describes the basic logic of what is now known as "multilevel selection." This refers to a way of quantifying how strong the selection pressure is at each level, which means how strongly the competition of life favors genes for particular traits (Bregman 2020). The most important "stimulus to the development of the social virtues" was the fact that people are passionately concerned with "the praise and blame of our fellow men" (Bregman 2020).

The advantages of group life may be so great that humans are biologically prepared to seek membership and avoid isolation. From an evolutionary psychology perspective, because groups have increased humans' overall fitness for countless generations, individuals who carried genes that promoted solitude-seeking were less likely to survive and procreate compared to those with genes that prompted them to join groups (Darwin 1871). This process of natural selection culminated in the creation of a modern human who seeks out membership in groups instinctively, for most of us are descendants of "joiners" rather than "loners."

Darwin believed that the emotions that drive our obsession with reputation were acquired by natural selection. When you put it together, if there is a genetic basis for the feelings of loyalty, then intense intergroup competition will make these genes become more common in the next generation. The theory goes a long way in explaining why people are groupish (Bregman 2020). It also has huge implications for why we feel obligated to take responsibility for our actions and behaviors.

Jobs Versus Roles

When we join an organization, we are given a job. A job is a defined part played by a person in an organization. Jobs should be guided by the decisions you make on the primary axis for your organization model. For example, if the decision was made that the winning characteristic of the organization was its ability to deliver efficient production of a single product with great service, then you may have a set of jobs focused on production and a separate set focused on customer service. Alternatively, if your core competency is to deliver customized solutions to unique customers, jobs will be based on customer segments. This might lead to groups of jobs focused on commercial customers and separate ones focused on retail consumers.

The assignment of people to jobs creates patterns of interaction that give reasons and motivation for people to interact and cooperate with a common purpose. For example, when someone within a group has a financial issue, they might initially talk to the treasurer of that group. Beyond that initial step, the treasurer may have reasons to engage with other jobs outside that group, such as with financial analysts or other jobs focused on financial matters.

Roles, in comparison, can be self-assumed when a person takes responsibility for a certain task or function within a group or acts in a way that creates a shared understanding related to the informal role. Typically, we all play multiple roles at work and in life. Your job might be "parent," but the roles you play on any given day might be chauffeur, nurse, teacher, and housekeeper.

People can also informally assign roles to others over time through patterns of interaction. For example, group members may come to know that if you need travel bookings, you go talk to Jane, even though her job is "office manager," not "travel coordinator." Roles create obligations and expectations and reinforce social identity, which in turn encourage actions that support group goals. Roles create tangible and powerful signals of social norms associated with the role. Roles often create bridging and linking ties that create opportunities to "get ahead."

These patterns of interaction create and strengthen social capital that can benefit the group, the actors, and the community more broadly. Social capital is built and manifested primarily by social interaction, so structures that create interaction, particularly between people who may otherwise not interact, are an important source of social capital. Clearly defined jobs allow people to work together predictably, fruitfully, and efficiently (Uphoff and Wijayaratna 2000). They are important for making decisions, mobilizing resources, communicating efficiently, coordinating activities, and resolving conflicts.

Allow me to share a rather embarrassing personal example of the difference between a job and a role. I was sitting on a plane next to a fellow passenger, and we politely introduced ourselves and where we worked. She shared that her job was product engineer at HP. When I later pulled out my computer to get some work done, I remembered that my laptop screen had dimmed the night before and I could not figure out why. She noticed that I was working on an HP, and excitedly said, "Don't you love the built-in privacy screen? I was the one who developed that feature!" I stared blankly at her for a moment, and then down at my computer, where I was surprised to find this very button, and with a single tap, my laptop screen immediately brightened. And I was thrilled that she had played that role at HP because she saved me from squinting my way through the flight (and possibly the days ahead).

Roles Versus Social Capital

Formal jobs are assigned to individuals at a specific level of the hierarchy and are associated with titles and compensation bands. Employment positions typically have a grade, job family, and designated place in the hierarchy, denoted with supervisor and subordinate relationships. Obligations regarding legal and regulatory compliance associated with the job are usually codified. A job grade will be associated with a specific salary band as well as eligibility for incentives, bonuses, benefits, and so on.

A role exists when there are shared and mutual expectations about what any person in a certain role should and will do under various conditions. This means that creating social capital requires more than just introducing roles, since it is the acceptance of roles that patterns people's behavior in predictable and productive ways. These expectations need to be shared by both role incumbents and those who interact with that role.

People both within and outside of the group tend to understanding what is normally appropriate and expected for a role (i.e., how someone in that role should act). This allows the efficient coordination of action with various benefits for social capital strengthening. Roles create various understandings that are necessary for people to work together on complex tasks. One of the few scholars to discuss how roles relate to social capital systematically was social scientist Norman Uphoff (Claridge 2004).

Another way to increase social capital is to implement shared or team goals. Goals are essentially mental models that allow individuals to depict, explain, comprehend, and predict events. Team goals must be perceived as important and achievable for organizations to get the benefit of increased social capital. Once these mental models can be shared by a group, they become a group-level phenomenon. The shared goal orientation becomes especially pivotal in uncertainty because it encourages adoption of these goals as they are in line with the norms, values, and beliefs of the group (Edmondson and Harvey 2017).

Social organization is less costly and often more effective in cases in which cooperation is motivated by norms, values, beliefs, and shared goals that create reinforcing expectations rather than having to gain cooperation through material incentives or coercive actions (such as those attained by hierarchical position). As Uphoff and Wijayaratna (2000) demonstrate in their study on social capital, "While such incentives and actions may be involved in any complex set of social relations, if they are all that produces intended behavior, this is a very expensive way to achieve results." Instead, understanding and investing in creating reinforcing expectations is the most effective way to create a sense of belonging.

But Does Belonging Really Matter in Business?

A 2019 study by the leadership development platform BetterUp found that workplace belonging can lead to an estimated 56% increase in job performance, a 50% reduction in turnover risk, and a 75% decrease in employee sick days. However, the study also found that a single incidence of "micro-exclusion" can lead to an immediate 25% decline in an individual's performance on a team project (BetterUp 2021). As social psychologists Roy Baumeister and Mark Leary conclude in their 1995 article, humans have "a pervasive drive to form and maintain at least a minimum quantity of lasting, positive, and impactful interpersonal relationships."

When we join a company, we are placed into a group. We become members in the formal hierarchy, such as a function like information technology or finance, or a division based on a location or a type of product or service. Most often it is both. Given our innate group tendency, we can almost immediately identify with these groups, and in doing so, we see other groups as potentially suspicious or as a source of competition.

We can leverage what we have learned thus far about the importance of belonging, the biological strength of membership, proximity, and shared fate to enhance how our organizations are designed. Earlier in this chapter, we learned about the many psychological systems that contribute to the effective tribalism and success in intergroup competition. We despise being lonely. We love local connections. We like little herds. In *Networks*, researcher Mark Newman (2020) says mini-tribes of 8–15 people are best. However, we have to be careful because in our small networks we have echoes, double counting, and people whose information might not be relevant.

What Does This All Mean for Organization Design?

Within a hierarchy, we create jobs. These are the primary places we find belonging, as we are attached to our business unit or function or geography. This job is a collection of tasks assigned to one position, with a defined reporting relationship. Classic job design focuses on top-down processes where leaders design their subordinates' jobs. As we have discussed, organizations, for the most part, cannot just have everyone be free to do whatever they want.

However, in today's complex environment, we need some degree of freedom. Rather than making formal changes to position descriptions and the structural characteristics of jobs, job crafting is a process whereby employees shift the task and relational boundaries of their jobs (Berg, Dutton, and Wrzesniewski 2001). Task crafting can alter the boundaries of a job by adding or subtracting tasks, expanding or reducing the scope of tasks, or changing how tasks get done (Berg, Dutton, and Wrzesniewski 2001).

In addition to task crafting, relational crafting involves initiative changes to the social features of working and pushing the relational boundaries of a job. It might involve creating new relationships, limiting or ending toxic interactions, or taking steps to cultivate and strengthen positive relationships at work. Further, employees might think about their work connections in a new way, potentially developing a greater sense of meaning and appreciation for the role that other people have in their work life. There is evidence that when job crafting occurs among work groups that collectively modify how their work is to be organized and enacted (also known as collaborative crafting), there is a positive relationship with job performance (Leana, Appelbaum, and Shevchuk 2009).

Today's work content is not fixed. Organization behavioral scientists Justin M. Berg, Amy Wrzesniewski, and Jane E. Dutton coined the term "adaptive moves" to describe an employee's ability to craft their job to the extent they believe they have the autonomy to make changes to their experience of work (Berg, Dutton, and Wrzesniewski 2001). In recalling the social determinant theory of human motivation, these needs are to feel autonomous, competent, and related to others. The impetus to engage in job crafting arises from these.

9

Responsibility

"The swings between centralization and decentralization at the top of large . . . corporations have resembled the movements of women's hemlines."
— Henry Mintzberg, *The Structuring of Organizations* (1979)

One of my favorite clients was a new COO in a large integrated health system. She had quickly come up with a list of improvements to make to the company's operations, with an early example being a simple tool to streamline resourcing that was an industry best practice and widely used at other similar health systems. Being new, she searched for the appropriate approval process and was pleased to find a governing body that reviewed and approved the implementation of the new tool.

However, she also found a couple of other leaders, committees, and governing bodies that this group wanted her to seek approval from as well. Slightly discouraged, she sought approval in a few more places. Slowly, she was able to present, discuss, and receive approval from these additional people and committees. But these approvals were conditional on her seeking approval from yet more people, and then some more.

Fast forward nine months and *45 approvals later*, she launched the implementation of this simple improvement tool. Unfortunately, after all of this, she was stopped dead in her tracks by a lone executive who had somehow been left off of the previous 45 approvals; they were just not sure they approved and wanted more time and information to decide. A year later, when my client quit this organization in frustration, the tool was still not approved or implemented. Why? Because it served these leaders to keep the decision rights murky so they would not have to forfeit their own decision authority over their area of the business for which they were held accountable.

Most organizations are structured around vertical functions or departments (e.g., sales, marketing, service, support). Many decisions cross these functional boundaries, requiring multiple people from different functions to agree. The main reason we have so many meetings is to bring these vertical functional silos together, because to make decisions or receive approvals, we need to include representatives from many different areas.

This becomes especially difficult if win–lose results or trade-offs are required. And becomes further amplified if your organization is risk-averse or if failure is not tolerated, because people do not want to take responsibility for another department's decision. They will send emails to cover themselves or organize meetings to make sure the relevant department signs off on the proposal, so that if anything goes wrong, it is not seen as their fault. This was certainly the experience of my COO.

Accountability, Authority, and Responsibility Defined

In determining the optimal way to make decisions, many theorists and business leaders focus on authority, accountability, and responsibility. Unfortunately, there is no common agreement in the business literature as to the meaning and use of these terms, and in the applied world, these terms are often used interchangeably and defined differently across different settings.

Some say accountability is literally the ability to account for or report an event or outcome. With this definition, the accountable person simply reports on the activity or the metric but does not take the credit or blame. While this may be definitionally correct, it does not fulfill the spirit of what we mean by accountability at work. We actually mean that for the scope of a particular role, there are expectations and consequences (good and bad) for the outcomes.

For our purposes, we will say accountability at work can be defined as individuals in roles and groups working in teams who are given ownership for their actions and the outcomes of these actions. If something goes wrong, they take the blame. If something goes right, they get the credit. Accountability is the basis for defining metrics and, ultimately, rewards systems.

The literature also suggests that a simple, enabling ladder of authority promotes the rise of accountability ladders. The authority ladder also appears to affect how people take accountability for various tasks and challenges. For this to work, subordinates must be granted the authority they require to complete a task—that is, the power to make the necessary decisions. In addition, they will need sufficient resources.

Does this type of interdependence tend to destroy accountability? We often hear managers say things like, "How can I be held accountable for results that depend on the performance of others?" The misconception present here is that we can be accountable for our work only if we are the sole authority over it and can control all the resources necessary to accomplish the task.

However, it is possible for a person to be accountable without having exclusive control over the resources needed to deliver, as long as others who have authority over those resources are willing to cooperate (Morieux and Tollman, 2014). It is about the power and effectiveness of people working together through connection and collaboration taking responsibility individually and collectively, rather than relying on traditional hierarchical status.

In hierarchy design, authority flows down and accountability flows up. In comparison, I define responsibility as something you feel is your duty, and you do it to increase trust within your networks. It means you do the things you are supposed to do. When you are irresponsible, you breed mistrust. When you are responsible, trustworthiness ensues. A person in a job with higher authority in the hierarchy can delegate accountability for outcomes. Whether or not you accept responsibility for this is up to you as an individual in your role or roles. Please see Table 9.1 for how this can work.

The art, then, of architecting an effective organizational decision system is the right mix of position authority and delegated accountability in the hierarchy, and fostering the right environment so people take responsibility in their networks. Once these structures have been designed, the next pieces of the puzzle must fit together to place accountability clearly. This is accomplished by thoughtful job and role design.

Table 9.1   Authority, accountability, and responsibility.

	Authority	Accountability	Responsibility
Meaning	Right to make decisions	Being answerable to outcomes	Obligation to perform tasks at an agreed-upon standard
Origin	Arises from position in the scalar chain	Arises from delegated authority	Arises from relationships
Flow	Flows vertically down the levels of hierarchy	Flows vertically up the levels of hierarchy	Flows horizontally across the network
Delegation	Can be delegated	It can be partially delegated	It cannot be delegated

Unleashing Autonomy

Research suggests that employee motivation is dampened when employees are ordered to undertake a particular task by superiors, but they are more likely to be committed when they have participated in a decision (Powell 1990). Organizations largely drawing on decision-making authority in the hierarchy tend to reduce intrinsic motivation, engagement, and responsibility among employees (Saks 2017). Similarly, economists Philippe Aghion and Jean Tirole (1997) observed that the more the rules of the hierarchy were limited, the more likely people were to claim more responsibility in their roles. Intrinsic responsibility and decision-making authority can thus freely flow in any direction (Aghion and Tirole 1997). When people have the decision-making power and the resources to work toward a meaningful purpose, they don't need pep talks or stretch targets.

Agricultural business, the Morning Star Company, is often cited as a good example of role autonomy, where actors take responsibility. Here you may hold 20 different roles, and for each one you specify what it does, what authority you believe it should have (recommend, decide, or a combination), what indicators will help you understand if you are doing a good job, and what improvements you hope to make on those indicators. You then negotiate these responsibilities upstream and downstream individually so that you can commit to those who are next in the chain and you have the commitments from those before you in the chain (Laloux 2014).

Figure 9.1 is a picture of the network of agreements between people. One could argue that every organization has a network structure that looks something like this: an intricate web of fluid relationships and commitments that people engage in to get their work done. The work going on in the web of relationships is clearly articulated and accounted for at this innovative company (Laloux 2014).

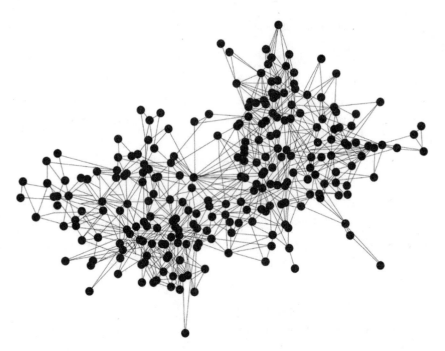

Figure 9.1   The web of commitments at Morning Star.

Source: Reinventing Organizations (Laloux, 2014 / Nelson Parker)

Aligning Decisions with the Hierarchy (Central Accountability) and the Network (Decentral Empowerment)

Despite calls for more self-management and emergent leadership (Laloux 2014), the vast majority of organizations continue to operate on the basis of an extensive chain of authority. Accordingly, when self-managing teams, mission-based teams, agile teams, or similar practices are introduced, the interplay between responsibility and authority ladders often becomes problematic. Solving this decision challenge organizationally will allow knowledge workers to thrive.

It is common today for decision-making to be pushed down to the front lines of the organization, the theory being that you can go faster with this structure. However, you can't do that with every decision. So how do you decide which ones to centralize? To answer

Table 9.2   Central and decentral trade-offs.

When it's important to be . . .	Responsive and innovative	Reliable and consistent
. . . it's usually best to place decisions . . .	Decentral	Central
. . . as this stimulates . . .	Immediacy	Compliance

this, each company has to think through which of these is most important to its business. As Table 9.2 shows, if reliability and consistency are more important, centralize; if responsiveness is everything, decentralize.

If customers, competitors, employees, regulators, and/or partners are genuinely different between business units, then it makes sense to locate these activities and the corresponding accountability for execution at that level. For some activities, it is necessary to have common policies, standards, methods, procedures, or systems to align the operating units with the overall enterprise objectives. A traditional economy of scale, where a unit does more of the same task, is one example. Minimum efficient scale, where you share deep, expensive expertise, is another. A third is avoiding duplication, when different units have a common need for which the solutions can be nearly identical.

Decision Bias

A chapter on decision-making in a book that designs organizations around how humans behave would not be complete if we didn't at least touch on decision bias. The concept was first introduced by researchers Amos Tversky and Daniel Kahneman (1979), which launched the field of behavioral economics, otherwise known as psychology. Since then, researchers have described a number of different types of biases that affect decision-making in a wide range of areas, including social behavior, cognition, behavioral economics, education, management, health care, business, and finance. In sum, humans are terribly flawed decision-makers.

Let's take a look at how decision bias clouds our logic when we have an organizational goal that we are accountable for achieving. One of the common biases—motivated reasoning—kicks in and impacts information-processing strategies the brain uses to make judgments and decisions. Specifically, information is processed in such a way that allows the decision-maker to believe the goal will be attained. As a result of this biased processing, information that supports a goal is given greater weight in the judgment process, while information that suggests a goal will not be reached is discounted. This bias leads us to be overconfident in our goal attainment (another bias), and as a result, we see things like missed project deadlines, overspending on transformations, and an escalation of commitment to initiatives that leads to "throwing good money after bad" (another bias—the sunk-cost fallacy).

Figure 9.2 is a classic example of anchoring bias in perception.

These behavioral biases impact our ability to make decisions about everything, including performance management, further strengthening the argument for giving up performance ratings from

Figure 9.2   How many ladies do you see?
Source: "My Wife and My Mother-in-Law," Public Domain / Library of Congress's Prints and Photographs division

Chapter 7: Measurement. For example, the halo (or horns) effect occurs when raters' perceptions of various aspects of performance are unduly influenced by their positive (or negative) perception of one aspect of performance: Raters or judges place too much weight on one aspect of performance and allow it to shape how they view overall performance quality.

Perhaps the most pervasive of all biases in terms of its impact on organizations is the confirmation bias, which is the very human tendency to seek out and remember information that confirms a previously held hypothesis or hunch. More than 180 cognitive biases have been documented in the literature (Desjardins 2021). The most troubling truth is that there is nothing to be done to overcome these biases at the individual level. Sure, we consultants can bring awareness to people, but people cannot stop these inherent flaws any more than they can stop being human. And, oh, by the way, cognitive rigidity gets amplified by time pressure, negative emotions, exhaustion, and other stressors—often the very conditions we are working in! Within organizations, then, what can be done?

Getting Decision Rights Right

The answer to overcome bias and improve decision outcomes in organizations is to intentionally design decision processes at the group and system level. A disciplined decision process is the best *way* to improve the quality of decisions and guard against common decision-making biases. Strategy, innovation, and decision scientists Dan Lovallo and Olivier Sibony studied 1,048 "major" business decisions over five years.

The results were surprising. Most business decisions were not made on gut calls but rather on rigorous analysis, yet they were poor decisions. In short, most people did all the legwork we think they are supposed to do—they delivered large quantities of detailed analysis (Lovallo and Sibony 2006). But this wasn't enough. In an article for *McKinsey Quarterly*, Lovallo and Sibony (2006) wrote, "Our research indicates that, contrary to what one might assume, good analysis in the hands of managers who have good judgment won't naturally yield good decisions."

The researchers also explored decision processes by asking respondents to "explicitly explore and discuss major uncertainties or discuss viewpoints that contradicted the senior leader's." So what matters more, process or analysis? After comparing the results, they determined that *process mattered more than analysis—by a factor of six*" (Lovallo and Sibony 2006).

There are not many places in business where we can improve a process and get a 600% improvement in an outcome. So, how are organizations doing? Well, 24% of US managers strongly agree that their peers make well-thought-out decisions. Even fewer managers (14%) strongly agree they are satisfied with the speed of decision-making at their organization. One thing is clear: Most organizational decision-making is still not working (Musser and Sundaram 2020).

One of my seasoned clients said they preferred to keep things "intentionally messy" to let their people "figure things out." Although the sentiment of self-discovery was appreciated, the time wasted making, remaking, and vetoing decisions was not as helpful as being intentionally clear in the first place. Unfortunately, most organizations sacrifice speed by taking a more-is-better approach to decision-making collaboration. Such behaviors can make leaders feel they are increasing alignment and organization focus on strategic objectives, when in fact they usually only create unmanageable collaborative demands and fail to bring about changes. A network perspective can help to rectify this unproductive approach by ensuring decision interactions within an organization are efficiently supporting strategic objectives (Cross, Thomas, and Light 2009).

What does a good decision process look like? As we will see in the next chapter, there is no one right process. The key is to have everyone agree to a process and follow it. Some leading-practice techniques can help combat bias, such as placing a devil's advocate in a group to take an opposing view to counter confirmation bias or "walking a mile in their shoes," where members of the group play different roles to widen their options and gain new perspectives. (These are perhaps best described by researchers Chip and Dan Heath in their book *Decisive* [2013].) And there are some common steps that most effective decision processes follow. Gallup created a simplified list based on extensive research (Musser and Sundaram 2020):

Foundation

1. Understand the purpose and nature of the required decision(s).
2. Use relevant and available data and inputs.
3. Involve the right people at the right times.

Development

4. Establish and adhere to pertinent decision-making procedures.
5. Clarify roles and responsibilities of all decision-making participants.
6. Foster an environment that encourages participants to share opinions and embrace healthy debate.
7. Ensure decision(s) made align(s) with organizational purpose, culture, and values.
8. Develop a plan of action.
9. Forecast the likely impact of the decision(s) and plan for contingencies.

Realization

10. Communicate the decision(s) to the right audiences.
11. Ensure follow-through.
12. Apply lessons learned to future decisions.

Decision Frameworks

Many organizations have pursued accountability by using a framework for decision-making. Often called "RACI" (responsible, accountable, consulted, and informed) or a similar acronym, frameworks like these attempt to clarify who makes what decisions and, frankly, who doesn't get to make decisions. Equally important are the decision-making and the decision-implementation processes that flow from this clarification in decision rights.

Over the years I have found that to optimize decision-making, a more simplified approach to empowering networks of teams works best. The position you hold as a leader in the hierarchy outlines your authority. You are free to delegate this authority. As a rule of thumb, you should keep about 25% of the decisions that matter and the rest you should empower others to make.

How do you decide when to keep a decision or when to delegate it? One idea is to keep for yourself those decisions with high negative or positive consequences for you and your organization. Another is to retain those decisions that require significant related experience and therefore have a high degree of conviction. Think risk management, ethics, brand, or other critical aspects that need to be consistently and uniformly managed centrally (see Table 9.3).

When the stakes are high and there is someone with more expertise who should own the decision, then you should delegate. Another situation occurs when you may be the expert, but the consequences are low, thus making it a great learning opportunity for another. Finally, if a decision is neither important nor in your area of expertise, it should be made by your team (see Figure 9.3) (Rabois 2016).

Table 9.3 When to delegate.

	High conviction	Low conviction
High consequence	Do it yourself	Delegate to a trusted expert
Low consequence	Delegate to develop others	Always delegate

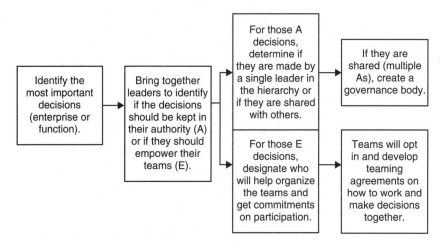

Figure 9.3   The authority/empowerment (A/E) exercise.

Responsibility will be cultivated in two ways: top-down executive understanding of which decisions will need to be held and which should be given to teams, and bottom-up teams working horizontally to solve issues.

It is important that you have a clear understanding of the process needed to get to a proper and efficient result. Otherwise, you will wind up in a morass of "approvals" that can number in the 40s and never get even the simplest of improvements implemented in your organization. No one wants that, and no one plans for that, but that is what happens if these ideas are not kept in mind.

In a recent executive workshop, we reviewed the top 25 decisions that matter and had the leaders work through the "A and E" exercise together like the one described in Figure 9.3. Upon completion, the executive team had assigned 100% of the accountability to the chief executive officer (CEO). The CEO was concerned and ultimately disappointed to learn that not a single other executive was willing or able to take any level of accountability for decisions being made. We needed to regroup as a team and form a more holistic teaming agreement and distribution of accountabilities, beyond the CEO.

Whether it is Gallup's checklist, a teaming agreement, or a governance charter, just like team norms, as long as the process is understood and followed, everybody wins.

Team Empowerment

Researchers Thomas and Velthouse describe empowerment as something that stimulates learning behaviors in self-managed teams. When teams have the latitude and the ability to experiment and implement potential solutions as they see fit, they are likely to learn as they go about accomplishing their work. In contrast, when groups are denied substantial freedom, they may fall into a firefighting mode of merely reacting to problems rather than pushing on toward a goal. Empowerment enables the expression of intrinsic motivation (Thomas and Velthouse 1990).

Motivation increases when individuals are given authority to make decisions (that is, when they have been delegated authority over certain tasks). Yet individuals only feel empowered when they are competent to make the decision delegated to them, and then they only feel comfortable being held accountable for the outcomes of those types of decisions (Edmondson and Harvey 2017). Team researchers have operationalized "empowerment by leadership" or granting team members the kind of autonomy that makes it more meaningful to complete skilled tasks and, thereby, boosts individual motivation, provided those team members believe they can impact the tasks over which they are given autonomy. Academic literature robustly demonstrates that the more people perceive they are autonomous, the more initiative they take in work-related situations. We further explore the development of teaming agreements in the next chapter, Teaming.

10

Teaming

"We learned that individual expertise did not distinguish people as high performers. What distinguished high performers were large and more diversified personal networks."
—Robert L. Cross, *The Hidden Power of Social Networks* (2004)

I was working on a challenging project with a complex global client operating in more than 100 countries with about 40 regional chief executive officers (CEOs). Each of these CEOs ran their region as a separate business with financial independence. In order to reduce costs and protect the global brand, the organization was attempting to implement a global set of standards, anchored on a standard technology. Each of the regional leaders had a slightly different client base and operating model, and each had slightly different perspectives on the importance of the global initiative. There were also legacy differences between the regional leaders (e.g., France and the United States) that made some of the interpersonal relations challenging.

As part of the program, our team highlighted all the key decisions that had to be made and where a consistent approach to process or technology had to be agreed upon. We then attempted to bring the leaders together to align on these big decisions but found we could not get out of the gate without the conversation devolving into a focus on differences. What was even more challenging was that no one actually had to agree—they could continue operating in silos without much in the way of negative repercussions.

While suboptimizing the enterprise, they were optimizing for their uniqueness. They were measured on their individual profit-and-loss (P&L), not on their collective contribution to the global brand, and as such, they were not incentivized to cooperate. When one of the large markets (say the United States) needed another country (say France) to operate in a consistent way, the leaders expended their own political capital to influence the outcome.

The result was a failure. After 24 months, a watered-down version of the technology was implemented in the United States and a 3-year roadmap for global implementation was designed, with the implementation still going on today (5 years later). This is a classic story of failure to team across different countries and businesses for the benefit of the enterprise.

Teams Versus Teaming

Teams are obviously critical for collective advancement. Today, Ernst and Young, LLP's People Advisory Services estimates that 65% of all of us in the workforce work on more than one team (internal research). One of those teams—at best—is in the organization chart, and the rest are not. Yet most, if not all, of our work happens on these different teams. To get a wise crowd, you need the right information in the first place and a well-balanced communication network. The recent experience with my global client's failed technology implementation illustrates the importance of teaming.

Despite what we have shown about the drawbacks of silos, in stable and enduring teams, we *can* get things done. We preferentially collaborate with the groups we feel we belong to, and our membership in these groups makes us feel engaged. In the case of a stable, well-bounded team in a single organizational area, norms and routines are largely defined by a shared and familiar context.

Historically, almost all team research has been done on solid, ongoing teams with clearly defined boundaries and objectives. However, in today's working worlds, we often don't have the luxury of stable teams. Most team diversity studies examine the effects of knowledge diversity in bounded and reasonably stable teams rather than individual collaboration in fluid arrangements or "fleeting team-like arrangements." With this new type of teaming, professional clashes are a barrier to growth and innovation. Teaming outside of this norm brings uncertainty; to combat this, we need an engaging vision, collectively built, where participants are focused on contributing to a common problem (Edmondson and Harvey 2017).

When Are Groups Wise?

Groups are wiser than people, provided there is no systematic bias. An essential task in any organization is processing and aggregating information from multiple sources, both internal and external (Jackson 2019). In *The Wisdom of Crowds*, journalist James Surowiecki (2005) describes wise crowds as having several key characteristics. First, the crowd should be able to exist even with a diversity of opinions. Secondly, one person's opinion should remain independent of those around them (and should not be influenced by anyone else). Next, anyone taking part in the crowd should be able to form their own opinion based on their individual knowledge. Finally, the crowd should be able to aggregate individual opinions into one collective decision.

Given what we now know about networks and membership, the just noted wiseness criteria are not so easy to achieve. Homophily, echo chambers, and unbalanced networks all create barriers. This is most likely why meta-analysis shows weak or inconsistent support for the assumption that the presence of knowledge diversity necessarily leads to better performance outcomes (Edmondson and Harvey 2017). Diverse knowledge is often underutilized on teams.

Key processes to leverage diversity continue to relate to the exchange, discussion, and integration of task-relevant information. However, today we participate on multiple teams, sometimes very infrequently or with fluid membership. When birds of a different feather must suddenly flock together, it doesn't always lead to better outcomes (Edmondson and Harvey 2017). Forgetting these basic network divides can lead one to propose ineffective policies when trying to fix such problems.

Boundary Spanning

Cross-boundary teams allow organizations to leverage the potential of innovation. Yet success of extreme teaming can be too easily thwarted by communication failures at the boundaries. Philosopher and political economist John Stuart Mill said two centuries ago, "It is hardly possible to overrate the value of placing human beings in contact with persons dissimilar to themselves, and with modes of thought and action unlike those with which they are familiar. . . . Such communication has always been . . . one of the primary sources of progress" (quoted in Edmondson and Harvey 2017).

This historic quote highlights what takes place at the intersection of knowledge domains. As we saw earlier, sociologist Ronald Burt calls these "structural holes" or gaps between two discrete groups with nonredundant knowledge. These act like insulators in an electric circuit in that knowledge within each group is buffered and develops within a distinct logic (Burt 2001). Innovation emerges from selection and synthesis across the structural holes between groups. Social network theory suggests that highly diverse teams can obtain valuable knowledge from interpersonal relationships outside the team.

It is difficult to transfer knowledge developed in one context and simply apply it to a new one (Burt 2001). Promoting shared mental models and bridging gaps in terminology, values, time frames, and tasks all lead to enhanced team performance. To be effective, there is a need to co-create common ground by developing a collective mental model. That said, seeing and appreciating the complementarity of diverse expertise can be elusive. Differences are more likely to produce conflict or misunderstanding than synergy. Therefore, teams must engage in perspective taking with one another to identify a shared mental model (Burt 2001).

Super Chickens

The bottom line regarding this idea is that work is social. In entrepreneur Margaret Heffernan's TED Talk, "Forget the Pecking Order at Work," she describes evolutionary biologist William Muir's experiment with chickens to see how to get more productive flocks (Hefferman 2015). Chickens live in groups, so he left one group alone for six generations. For a second group, he chose "super chickens" that were individually the most productive and put them together in a "super flock." He did this for each generation, and after six, he observed that egg production had increased dramatically in the first group. In the second group, however, all but three "super chickens" were dead because they had pecked the rest of the flock to death.

The findings indicated that the only way to be successful in the super chicken group was by suppressing the productivity of others. For the most part, this describes how organizations are designed today. We run organizations like the super chicken case. To get ahead, you must compete. It's me or you—for me to succeed, you must fail.

This flies in the face of what we know about successful teaming. At the Massachusetts Institute of Technology, researchers did a study to figure out what makes successful teams (Hefferman 2015). Really successful teams showed high degrees of social sensitivity to each other. They gave roughly equal time to each other, and they had more women in them. The researchers found that the key is their social connectedness, so what happens between people is what really counts for performance much more so than any individual's talent, regardless of a person's talent level. Hefferman concludes that it's the mortar, not the bricks, that makes organizations successful. This ties back to the shift from a focus on human capital to social capital.

Think back to Darwin's multilevel selection theory (discussed in Chapter 8), and we see evolutionary support for these modern findings that groups find a way to suppress individual selfishness. When groups compete, the cohesive, cooperative group wins.

Big Potential

Author Shawn Archer (2018) in his book *Big Potential* reinforced Darwin's claim that it is not survival of the fittest but more survival of the best fit. Based on his Harvard student success study, he concludes, "While it would seem that those who would succeed were the superstars who could shine the brightest, in reality, the flashes of brilliance were actually coming from those who had found their place within a constellation of stars . . . with powerful implication of how we think about potential within our companies, our teams, and in our . . . careers" (p. 33).

Another good example is Google's Project Aristotle. Its mission was simple: build the perfect team. Google analyzed an incredible amount of data, including tens of thousands of responses across 180 teams, and the conclusion was astonishing. There was nothing showing that a mix of specific personality types or skills or backgrounds made any difference. The "who" part of the equation didn't seem to matter. "At Google, we're good at finding patterns," one lead Google researcher stated in a *New York Times* interview. "There weren't strong patterns here" (Duhigg 2016).

The conclusion? There is no perfect performer at the individual level. Individual traits and aptitudes are not predictors of success on a team. The company known best for searching for patterns could not find a pattern in which individual skills predicted the success of an individual on a team. And yet the "who" is what we mistakenly focus on in admission files, on job applications, in interviews, and in performance evaluations. We focus on human capital, not social capital, to our own detriment.

So what does predict success? The ecosystem around you is the best indicator. This can be assessed by measuring a group's collective intelligence. More specifically, this includes awareness of the importance of social connections (social sensitivity) and whether the team cultivated an environment where each person had an equal chance to speak and everyone felt safe sharing their ideas. The other factor in higher collective intelligence is the number of women on the team. Having slightly more women than men on a team improves the team's social sensitivity score (Duhigg 2016). High group or collective intelligence continually delivers higher success rates than a team of individual geniuses. These findings have been repeated multiple times with consistent outcomes.

To better understand how to measure and predict collective intelligence (CI), Riedl et al. (2021) used meta-analytic methods (a study of studies) to evaluate data collected in 22 studies, including 5,349 individuals in 1,356 groups, and found strong support for a general factor of CI. Furthermore, the data demonstrated that group collaboration processes were about twice as important for predicting CI than individual skill.

Size Matters

Gore-Tex was founded by Bill Gore. Gore had worked for Dupont previously and was struck by how dysfunctional big organizations were, especially the presence of siloed echo chambers within the company that refused to talk to each other. He felt that 150 people was as large as manufacturing organizations should get. He would build a second plant next to the first one rather than expand to a higher number. He felt that an organization did not need a lot of titles or job descriptions because at that number everyone knows who everyone is. He called it "flat lattice," or basically independent units scattered with a single strategic intent.

This is precisely why so many startups experience growing pains as they grow beyond 150 employees. For example, a well-known tech startup that we worked for used to have Monday meetings where the top execs got together to share ideas and lay out a plan for the week. As they grew, the meeting got larger and larger, spilling out of the conference room, with individuals sitting on the floor outside. In short order, instead of an informal and agile touch-base, all the chiefs of staff and team members spent their Sundays prepping for the

Monday meeting, carefully crafting every word. As the company grew exponentially, leaders eventually came to realize the time spent preparing and the meetings themselves were no longer adding value. Happily, the meetings were abandoned in their entirety and smaller subgroups formed. The smaller group size allowed these weekly huddles to return to their original value.

Perhaps Gore had stumbled upon an evolutionary truth. According to British anthropologist Robin Dunbar, the magic number of people in a network is 150. Dunbar became convinced that there was a ratio between brain sizes and group sizes through his studies of nonhuman primates. This ratio was mapped out using neuroimaging and observation of time spent on grooming, an important social behavior of primates. Dunbar concluded that the size, relative to the body, of the neocortex—the part of the brain associated with cognition and language—is linked to the size of a cohesive social group. This ratio limits how much complexity a social system can handle.

According to Dunbar and many researchers he influenced, this rule of 150 remains true for early hunter-gatherer societies as well as a surprising array of modern groupings: offices, communes, factories, residential campsites, military organizations, eleventh-century English villages, even Christmas card lists (Dunbar 2022). Exceed 150 and a network is unlikely to last long or cohere well. According to the theory, the tightest circle has just five loved ones. That's followed by successive layers of 15 good friends, 50 friends, 150 meaningful contacts, 500 acquaintances, and 1,500 people you can recognize. People migrate in and out of these layers, but the idea is that space has to be carved out for any new entrants.

What Does This All Mean for Organization Design?

Let's say I need help with something at work, and I get this help from my colleagues with no backstabbing or turf guarding. We have much higher social capital than a company fraught with territorial scheming, malice, and political infighting. So, if two companies are identical, but one has more social capital, that company is going to beat out the other. Higher social capital translates into higher productivity and higher flexibility. Because you are a team, you are one. It is also a lot more fun to work in a place where you work as a team (Haidt 2012)!

Social capital refers to the trust found in relationships. Researcher Amy Edmondson showed successful teams increased trust by creating decision clusters. They did this by allocating decision rights over tasks that did not require cross-boundary efforts, empowering experts to proceed independently, giving them autonomy within their area of expertise, and then ensuring coordination between areas of expertise (Edmondson and Harvey 2017). The introduction of modular work or tasks that can be accomplished independently in a complex team endeavor helps mitigate uncertainty by reducing the number of interconnections affected by future changes in a single aspect of the output (Edmondson and Harvey 2017). Diagnosing interfaces is meaningful when a decision affects more than one area of expertise. This is because knowledge is socially embedded and context-dependent.

Teaming agreements are an effective and inexpensive way to codify team norms regarding team behaviors and team decision-making processes. Using network insights, we can bring the right networks of teams together and provide these teams the tools to facilitate their own group process.

Another way to build social capital is through team incentives. Earlier in the book, we referenced "On the Folly of Rewarding A, While Hoping for B," written by Steven Kerr, former president of the Academy of Management (1995). It continues to be discussed and reprinted today, given its relevance to modern organizational challenges. Kerr comments on the folly of rewarding individual effort when we hope for teamwork. If success hinges on effective communication and collaboration across institutions but the workers in the institutions in question are responding to their own individual reward structures, effective collaboration is relatively unlikely.

Understanding what impacts our ability to improve the collective intelligence of a modern team allows us to build and harness social capital. In a working world where we sit on multiple teams a day, perhaps dozens overall, intentionally building social capital is the key to unlocking human potential at work. We can use our insights on hierarchy and networks to intentionally design collaboration between roles on teams, put the right teams together based on size and relationships, and empower these teams with clarity on decision-making and shared rewards. All of this creates a context that gives us a sense of belonging because we feel like we are members of groups in meaningful ways.

11 | Purpose and Utility

"All models are wrong, but some are useful."
—G.E.P. Box, "Robustness in the Strategy of
Scientific Model Building" (1979)

How does all of this work in the real professional world? Are these merely abstract thoughts or can we achieve concrete solutions by implementing the Peopletecture Model?

In my experience, two macro-level choices must be made in any organizational form that will lead to the plethora of architectural decisions that ultimately create a great organization:

1. What is the purpose of your organization? Why does it exist? Whom does it help? What is it all about?
2. What use will your organization's customers or clients derive from your product or service? What makes your organization's offerings unique? Why will people choose your business over your competitors'?

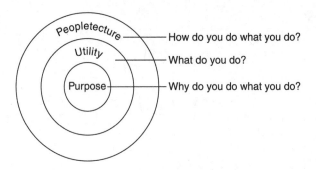

Figure 11.1   Purpose, utility, and architecture and how they interrelate.

Source: Tiffany McDowell

When these questions are answered clearly, there is a relatively straightforward path with regard to architecture. This means that those who build the organization's vertical and parallel structures should understand how to proceed to maximize the overall opportunity for growth and advancement.

To use an everyday example, when building a house, the purpose of the dwelling defines what value the user will derive, which tells the architect what to design. Ultimately, this translates to how the inhabitants feel and act in a structure (Bodan, Dickau, and Mullady 2020).

You'll see this laid out in Figure 11.1. We will delve into each of these choices and how they play out in organizations.

Purpose

The first decision is your "why" or your unique purpose and how that fits within the broader ecosystem. This describes your aspiration and cuts across all that you do. Examples are statements, such as Apple's "challenge the status quo" or Uber's "set the world in motion."

Based on what you hope to achieve, you can create value in different ways. There has been a renewed focus on purpose in the recent management literature, and it is an important way to inspire people about your organization—both employees and customers.

Purpose helps team members interpret their organization as an entity of significance, value, and worth. If we architect the organization correctly, members should be able to find personal meaning within the organization's purpose. This kind of meaning leads to higher levels of commitment and attachment, more people working on behalf of the institution over and above what is expected, and lower levels of turnover (Dutton 2020).

Organizational purpose is necessary, but it's not sufficient for employees to feel like their work has meaning. To have teams and individuals internalize the company purpose, we need the other elements of value and architecture to work in concert.

Utility

Your second decision relates to the "how" aspect of your overall mission, and here there are a wide array of basic ecosystem choices. You can set up a traditional, stand-alone organization and focus within your four walls. You can also choose different business models, such as joint ventures with other organizations, perhaps using a platform to reduce the complexity of contracting and increasing the ease of transacting with others. You can set up an open-source arrangement, where individuals and groups join the organization voluntarily and contribute what they like, when they like, à la Wikipedia. You can look at the capabilities of other individuals, groups, and companies and collaborate across these networks in the ecosystem, determining which capabilities you will focus on, which ones you will partner with others on, and which ones you will either buy or sell to.

Many of these more sophisticated options did not exist prior to the Information Age, when the ability to find and connect with different ecosystem players was bound by constraints such as geography. Making these ecosystem choices is an ongoing effort that requires a deep appreciation of the complexity of the markets around the globe. Ultimately, these choices will lead to success or failure.

These decisions, while critical for organizational life, are almost always made at inception by a handful of people, such as the founder or chief executive officer (CEO) with a few trusted advisors. They may be occasionally revisited by key advisors. The decision to recast the entire business model is also made fairly infrequently. While critically important, the vast majority of the people in the organization work according to these purpose and value choices that have already been made. It's like a fish describing water.

If you don't know the story, two young fish are swimming along, and they happen to meet an older fish swimming the other way, who nods at them and says, "Morning, boys, how's the water?"

The two young fish swim on for a bit, and then eventually one of them looks over at the other and asks, "What the heck is water?"

There is an order to these choices, which is best captured in Roger Martin's Integrated Strategic Choice Cascade, first published in *Playing to Win: How Strategy Really Works* (Lafley and Martin 2013). The simple question you need to answer is, "Based on our aspiration, where will we play and how will we win?" This is your essential intent, and it is both meaningful and measurable. (See Figure 11.2.)

Private, public, majority share/minority share—in our real estate metaphor, this is where you stake your territory. Regardless of the choices you make in the dizzying array of business model options (from a holding company to a fully integrated operating company), at some point you will land on the optimal way to achieve your purpose at that moment in time and then turn your attention to figuring out how you will operate your business.

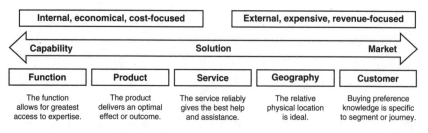

Figure 11.2   Utility characteristics.

We have just described business model choices, but many authors and practitioners mix up business model, operating model, and organizational model. This is unfortunate because when a term like "operating model" can mean everything, it then means nothing. So let's define it here once and for all.

In the operating model, you need to decide who are the people and what are the processes and technology needed to deliver on your purpose and value. Within the people part of the model, there are choices on organization and choices on workforce. In this book, we are focused on the organizational choices.

Primary Axis

Following the choice cascade, the next question is: What capabilities must be in place? These are your macro model choices, the "big rocks" that will set the frame for architecting the organization's context. At the highest level, there are really only three distinct ways to put an organization's hierarchy together to deliver the value your business model is predicated upon (albeit with some variations), as outlined in Figure 11.2.

The three ways to construct the top of the hierarchy (the primary axis) where you will place your executive leaders are:

- **Capability**—Define your functional orientation.
- **Solution**—Define your product and/or service or a combination of products and services to get to a set of solutions.
- **Market**—Define your geographic reach or customer by segmentation or life cycle.

The key in determining the primary axis for optimal utility is in answering this question: What capabilities must we have to win? If you get right down to it, what is your core competency that makes you unique? Is it how your customers view your deep capability and how your employees see themselves in their profession (like engineering, nursing, etc.)? Is it how your customers get a problem solved or an experience delivered through your unique combination of products, services, and solutions, or is the primary source of value knowing your markets and your customers? This is your core competency.

A core competency is a concept in management theory that is the foundation of companies' competitiveness. This concept, now widely applied in all strategy discussions, was introduced by Professor C. K. Prahalad and Gary Hamel, founder of the Management Lab, in their 1990 article "The Core Competence of the Corporation."

Core competencies fulfill three criteria:

1. They provide potential access to a wide variety of markets.
2. They should make a significant contribution to the perceived customer benefits.
3. They are difficult for competitors to imitate.

The recent book *Networked, Scaled, and Agile*, by consultants Amy Kates, Greg Kesler, and Michele DiMartino, does a great job of summarizing the key questions to help determine your primary value choices. They are paraphrased below (Kates and Kesler 2020):

- What is the ecosystem in which the business operates?
- What capabilities will deliver the most value to customers?
- What capabilities should be cultivated within the organization, and what should be outsourced or contracted?
- Where do we need integration, and where do we want separation?

Traditionally, most organizational strategists, C-suite leaders, and management consultants have stopped here with their line of inquiry for the enterprise model. However, the value to team members—not just customers and ecosystem partners—is missing from this standard question list. The following questions must also be answered to create the optimal model to achieve value for both customers and employees:

- Where should we standardize capabilities (since consistency is valuable)?
- Where should we encourage innovation (since new ideas and agility are valuable)?
- Where do we want our team members to feel their primary sense of belonging, their "home base"?
- What capabilities will our team members naturally gravitate toward?

These additional questions and subsequent decisions allow you to design for the behaviors you want to encourage. This ultimately shows how to structure your hierarchy so that it will be efficient, have little ambiguity, and require little invention. Instead, it will run smoothly because the members will know what to expect and be able to navigate using standard procedures, documented processes, learning programs, etc.

Recall from Chapter 6: Hierarchy Versus Networks that each layer in the structure must be uniquely value-adding, as hierarchical structure is most useful when it defines the space of potential interaction partners through organizational boundaries. This is really the first choice as to what is most uniquely value-adding, then all the other choices on how to structure reporting relationships, levels of reporting, and so on flow from this primary decision.

So What Is the Problem?

Let's say we have pondered our organization model choices and determined that "solution" is the optimal primary organizing characteristic. What do we mean by solution? Well, in a life sciences company, the solution could be to bundle drugs and drug delivery into one therapeutic area to treat certain cancers. In banking, the solution could be to bundle different lending and investment products and services to solve a customer challenge, such as buying a first home. In a technology company, the solution could be to bring together traditional products with new applications, like a watch with a blood pressure monitor.

We determine how many solutions we will have and, therefore, how many leaders we will need to lead each of these solutions based on size, complexity, and so on. But in today's complex, global, multidimensional businesses, it is neither realistic nor recommended to choose only one of the three dimensions of the organization model and exclude solving for the others. By far the most common value model is a hybrid or a multidimensional model that combines different aspects of the three dimensions just noted.

Almost all organizations of a certain size have chosen the hybrid model, as they believe it allows them to maximize all the possible value of their core competencies (e.g., solution and geography). In our previous examples, perhaps each country around the globe has a different regulatory environment that requires customization of the therapeutic areas, the banks deliver their homebuyer solution customized to their local branch customers, and the technology company has a sales team that focuses on regional markets to get its solutions into customers' hands.

Unfortunately, as we described earlier in the chapter on hierarchy, this has led to the implementation of multiple profit-and-loss accountabilities and of matrix reporting structures, which in turn have created unnecessary complexity that is not rewarded by the market. And since the market will not pay for this unnecessary complexity, the employees end up bearing the brunt of it, leading to friction, frustration, and, eventually, disengagement and burnout. This antiquated and failed reporting solution should be abolished, in my opinion.

Why? Because I have never seen matrix or dotted-line reporting work in my 20 years of organization design consulting. It has always struck me as an illogical solution to the problem we are trying to solve, since it destroys the elegance of the chain-of-command principle. We want our people to focus on their capability or business area, but we also want them to collaborate with and serve other parts of the organization by bringing them this capability. This is the same behavior we want from our employees serving our customers, but we don't require our people to have a dotted-line reporting to our customers in order to know how to collaborate.

Recall from the start of the book that matrix reporting takes a toll on people by harboring ambiguity and unclear expectations. A matrix structure gives rise to a lack of clarity about responsibilities and expectations. Instead, we now know that once we choose a primary value and use that axis to design our hierarchy, then the rest of our value attributes are solved by structuring the horizontal network of relationships. Silos actually have a place in organizations. Structure separates people into teams with shared mental models and measurements that allow them to work well together. If you change the primary axis to a different axis, you will simply get new silos.

Our focus here is on designing the optimal hierarchy, which is important but dwarfed with respect to how important it is to optimally structure the network. Thus, the balance of the characteristics will be structured in the network. We have already decided services are our primary axis. Let's say we are going to have geography as our secondary characteristic. We will intentionally structure the roles on these horizontal networks of teams using network science. For example, we could find some of the services team in the United States and connect them to a services team in the United Kingdom. We can calculate which roles would be best to connect and design their work so that they can share knowledge and best practices between the two countries.

Business history and organizational theory make the case that as entrepreneurial firms grow large and complex, they must shift from a functional to a multidivisional structure to align accountability and control and prevent the congestion that occurs when countless decisions flow up the org chart to the very top. Giving business unit leaders full control over key functions allows them to do what is best to meet the needs of their individual units' customers and maximize their results, and it enables the executives overseeing them to assess their performance. The few but compelling examples of this, like Apple, mentioned earlier, prove that this conventional approach is not necessary and that the functional structure may benefit companies facing tremendous technological change and industry upheaval (Podolny and Hansen 2020).

A Note on Front and Back Office

In most literature on organization model types, there is a delineation between "front" and "back" office. The front office is defined as the part of the company that meets clients or customers, such as sales and service. It is the face of the company. The back office is defined as the work that supports the front office and is not client facing. In almost all cases in organizations at scale (think 1,000 people or more), decision-makers quickly realize that back–office capabilities are best streamlined and standardized. As such, they are organized hierarchically by functional area. Thus, when designing the hierarchy of the back office, the question becomes less about choosing the value lever for corporate support functions and more about how to group or arrange the functions.

Figure 11.3 is a visual of the types of choices in arranging capabilities for value.

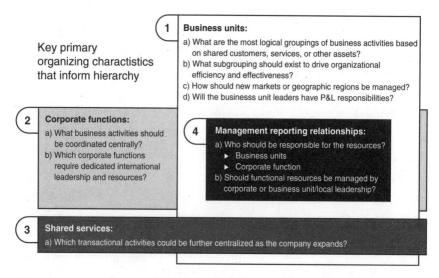

Figure 11.3   Arranging hierarchy for value.

Even within this framework of value choices for the front and back office, a plethora of options remain on how to group the specific capabilities. It is perhaps easiest to decide these by understanding there are really *only four moves you can make* within the hierarchy. You can

1. combine things,
2. split them apart,
3. elevate them to the management level, or
4. push them down to the team level.

Let's take a classic functional corporate design for a back office. Often, we ponder how best to combine these functional capabilities. In one option, we could combine different corporate support services into a single administrative function—a chief administrative officer who reports to the CEO. In this option, we would push down all the discrete corporate support services like information technology (IT), human resources (HR), and legal under this single functional leader. Alternatively, in a second option, we could break the capabilities apart and elevate the distinct functions, so we could have IT, HR, and legal in separate functions, each with an executive reporting to the CEO, typically the chief information officer, the chief human resources officer, and the chief legal officer, respectively.

Note, again, these are all choices we are making on hierarchy. The rest of the choices we make are on how to structure the network. There will be lots of ways to team across the enterprise. IT will support employees with their technology needs. HR will help managers coach and mentor their people in positive and engaging ways. Legal will advise executives on the best course of action for their particular business needs. And based on what we are trying to accomplish—speed, growth, innovation, flexibility, or efficiency—we will intentionally design these networks to achieve these business goals.

Case in Point

The value choices discussed previously are a critical input in designing an effective organization, and once they are made, the architect can get to work creating the system that will make the purpose and value come to life. Perhaps a short story from one of my great friends in organization design will drive home the point on value. My colleague joined a large global firm, and only weeks into his role, the CEO unexpectedly called him into a room in front of the whole executive team.

"We hired you because of your organization design expertise, so what structure is best for us?"

My friend is a professional, but I imagine he was sweating a bit. However, true to his nature, he replied, "I don't yet know. You have hired a tailor to stitch you 'the perfect garment.' However, you have not told me yet, do you want a skirt? A suit? Who will wear it? Do you want it out of silk to stand out at a formal event? Cotton to be functional and comfortable? Until you decide what you value—its function, fabric, and use—I cannot design your organization."

"The perfect garment" he mentioned connotes the purpose of the organization. As you can see, this is the methodology that needs to be implemented not just with new and young organizations but with all organizations. The same variables need to not only be evaluated but identified before any evaluation can even occur.

Like my friend, I have had many requests to design organizations. A typical client will ask me something like the following:

"Hi, great news! The CEO approved the new venture in Asia, and we have selected the perfect leader for the job. Can you get back to me with a draft organization structure, roles, and talent profiles? Preferably by next week?"

Or:

"We are facing some financial head winds this quarter; I need to get 5% labor costs cut and fast. What roles should I remove, how should I redistribute the work, and what will my team look like when we are done?"

Or:

"Surprise! We have to stop the project we are working on. We just bought our competitor, and we need to figure out the new operating model for the combined entity. It's unclear who will make the final decisions, but we need to get the organization model agreed upon ASAP, as we have targets to meet, and we need to keep all the great talent we just acquired and keep our shareholders happy! Can you help?"

To each of these I say, "Yes! But first, let's articulate the purpose and utility of the organization, then I will be happy to architect a design that will make you and your people flourish."

In an example more aligned to architecture as we usually think of it, let's examine the purpose of a building. Is the building meant to serve as modern high-rise apartments for young, single professionals? Is it a single-family dwelling for a multigenerational family? Is it low-cost housing for people experiencing homelessness to improve community health outcomes?

If you call and ask me to design the perfect building, I will say I am happy to do so, but first I'm going to have two initial questions:

1. Why do you need a building (what is its purpose)?
2. What is the building for and who will use it (what is its value)?

After you have made the initial choice, the fun part of designing begins—Peopletecture.

Earlier in this chapter, I introduced Roger Martin's Integrated Strategic Choice Cascade, which has five questions. We looked at the first four, and now we have reached the last question: What management systems are required? In my friend's metaphorical example, if we now know we are designing a formal suit in silk, then we begin drafting the pattern, arranging the pieces, and carefully sewing them together. For my examples, we deploy the Peopletecture Model.

The answers to these organizational model questions allow you to actually deliver the capabilities needed to win in your chosen sphere. That's because these Peopletecture choices that create individual and group experiences in turn help predict their engagement and performance. These are also choices that in practice tend to be revisited and changed much more frequently and by many more people in the organization than the first two macro decisions, which leads us to an important topic that has been missing in our Peopletecture Model thus far—what about the actual people?

Leadership, Experience, and Culture

I once heard a statistic that there are more than 15,000 books on leadership in print. While I have not read them all, the prevailing wisdom tells us that leadership is a causal variable in organizational performance, that people "join organizations and quit leaders," that they "look in the mirror before they look around," and even that the best leaders "eat last." Yet it greatly pains me that many researchers and practitioners leave the effort to work horizontally up to the individual. For example, some say the ability to collaborate effectively in the network is based on individual characteristics or skill, saying, "In order for the horizontal roles to be successful . . . leaders muster influence through knowledge, energy, vision, and persuasive communication" (Kates and Kesler 2020).

To be fair, when shifting from a more traditional hierarchal "command-and-control" type of organization design to one with a focus on empowering horizontal networks of teams, many leaders struggle with the new behaviors. New roles in the networks bring new authority and empowerment, and leaders often struggle to move from "I call all the shots" to "I guide the team to make the call." This increased focus on cross-unit collaboration is not a new idea. In the 1980s, the concept of the "T-shaped" leader became popular as more and more global companies put complex matrixed reporting in place.

In the vertical part of the letter T, you drive performance in the area you lead, and the horizontal part of the T is where you reach across internal boundaries to collaborate.

While there is no doubt that we can all improve, learn, grow, and become more impactful in our work in ourselves, our teams, and in our organizations, evidence is limited that individual leadership characteristics or behaviors impact an enterprise's overall performance in a sustained and meaningful way. Throughout this book, I have shared ample evidence that individual characteristics are not predictive of group or enterprise performance. Leaders are not an exception.

However, when leaders at all levels (meaning leaders in title as well as all employees who lead their work and collaborate with their colleagues) help craft and then uphold a context that is designed for humans to flourish, positive results occur. As researchers showed in a meta-analysis, people who feel they get the support they need at work do their jobs to the best of their abilities (Harter 2020). In fact, research repeatedly shows that in companies where senior leadership actually applies the principles we have described in Peopletecture, their people are more productive, engaged, and committed. They are also less likely to be absent or to have accidents, and they are more likely to stick with the organization as it copes with a demanding and ever-changing future (Harter 2020). And, lo and behold, research shows that such companies have higher levels of customer satisfaction and profits (Schneider 2021)!

The other important variable in leadership and followership is consistent, transparent communication. Organization psychologist Ben Schneider found the lead antecedent of work engagement was the regularity and clarity with which leadership communicated who they were and where they were headed with their employees. Work engagement was a statistically significant correlate of organizational financial performance (net margin and return on assets), customer satisfaction (the American Customer Satisfaction Index), and corporate reputation (the Harris Reputation Quotient) 1 and 2 years later for 102 companies from diverse industries (Schneider 2021).

So, having a purpose and communicating present and future value really does improve business outcomes.

A quick note on corporate culture. There is much talk today of "a culture of accountability." In fact, culture is simply an outcome measure of purpose, utility, and the six elements of Peopletecture. Culture can be described as the perceptions employees develop about how their organization functions and what it values (Schneider 2021). An organization's culture is the result of the decisions made on the six elements of Peopletecture. Through the application of the Peopletecture principles, such as the right roles, incentives, and delegated authority with real empowerment, leaders can connect people and teams with purpose for speed, innovation, growth, and scaling of best practices—all while preserving accountability.

Transformation Realized

In a recent study, the EY organization and Oxford University demonstrated that putting humans at the center of a transformation can improve the odds of success by more than *two and a half times* (Dutta and Gardner 2022). One of the key findings in the study, which focused on uncovering the emotional journey of leaders and teams, was that knowing how to build an environment where collaboration and accountability thrive led to sustained performance and engagement.

This significant finding indicates that among successful transformations, the search for new ways of working was deliberate and consciously involved leaders, teams, and individuals at all levels. One key tenet was that these organizations knew how to architect the infrastructure to enable the workforce to respond positively to change. This included clarifying decision rights and decentralized decision-making authority to avoid upward delegation.

In the best outcomes, teams were empowered to redesign their own work by consciously building interdependencies among teams. Leaders set boundaries for alignment across the organization, to manage both the emotional and political aspects of change (White 2022). This breakthrough study provides direct evidence for the power of Peopletecture. We use network theory to propose how a network structure enables—and disables—interactions between parties so that we intentionally structure interactions to achieve desired transformation outcomes.

For example, what effects do the marketing department's network and network interactions with sales have on interactions with the research and development department? Using network metrics, we can determine whether alternate structures of interdependence could produce the same or better outcomes while distributing power structure in different ways. We can look at where organizations are vulnerable to coordination-related failures and, knowing this, what interactions might be structured to produce the best business outcomes.

12

Peopletecture for Individuals and Managers

"People don't resist change; they resist being changed."
—Peter Scholtes, Brian L. Joiner, and Barbara J. Streibel,
The Team Handbook, 3rd ed. (2003)

My client, the head of all the commercial business units for a large insurer, right-hand advisor, and next in line to the chief executive officer (CEO), looked pointedly at me through the video screen. "I am just really worried about leading through this level of change for the organization." I nodded understandingly, having already had the "change experience" conversation with the chief human resources officer and with the project management lead of the reorganization project earlier that week.

This was not a conversation I was unfamiliar with. In fact, I cannot think of a single organization design project I have led that did not have a significant change and engagement effort associated with implementing the new design. No matter the level of the leader or the size of the reorganization effort, at a certain point the strategy-to-structure work becomes very human.

We were two months into an enterprise-wide organization transformation effort. This client had followed my Peopletecture Model to the letter. They were keen to protect the "connective tissue" that had been developed over a long period, while restructuring to forge new relationships essential to future business growth. To do this, they used network analysis to inform their changes to their hierarchy (from geography to solution). We carefully designed their new measurement system to incentivize the right behaviors from the top down, and they had a new decision and governance model that empowered their managers and front lines to best serve their customers. They had a plan to cascade the new design to their teams and engage each team in role crafting and in designing their team's empowerment model. "Tell me more about your concerns," I prompted her. And, as expected, the flood gates opened.

"Well, first there is Jamal. He is not going to like giving up his role as the Boston office leader. I know that it's not material to his performance or compensation, but it's a title that gives him credibility with his clients and with our people, and he is going to see this as a negative and could even leave if we aren't careful.

"Then there is Tatiana. She is going to be furious that she has to work with Sarah in her new role. Even though she had some mixed feedback on her performance, she is a more tenured leader than Sarah, and she is probably going to freak out that they are working side-by-side in the new model.

"Then there is the whole operations team, who have been reporting locally and now will have a new boss and new responsibilities. I know what you are going to say, that this is such a positive for these resources in terms of career opportunity, learning and growth, and camaraderie on teams, but it's still a big change. And people at our company really don't like change!

"These are just a few that are top of mind, but almost everyone will be impacted in some way, and while the lion's share of these changes are very positive for our people, it's So. Much. Change. I am just really worried about change management!"

I wanted to reach through my computer screen and give her shoulder a squeeze, knowing that this type of anxiety at this juncture was normal and to be expected. It showed she cared about her people and her organization. At a certain point, after moving from strategy to structure to talent, the conversation always becomes very much about the people.

"We are at the exact right time to have this conversation, now that we are ready to cascade the design to broader groups of your folks. We have a thoughtful and thorough plan prepared to engage all your different constituents in the right way and the right time. This will now become their design to own and implement.

"You as a senior executive are key to inspiring your teams with the future and all the benefits that will come from the changes in roles, reporting, teaming, and what that will lead to for meaning and belonging for individuals in their careers. But you are not alone! Now that we understand who the influencers are in the network across all your different teams, we will arm them with information to share with their teams. And we are empowering the teams to own the design and implementation!"

We had worked through role crafting and the accountable/empower framework with her and her executive team a few weeks prior. The plan was to follow this same approach in a cascaded fashion with directors, managers, and supervisors so that every person had the opportunity to have input on the roles they would play in the new structure, and so everyone understood what they were empowered to do as individuals and with their teams. "I think you will find that people might actually LIKE change when they get to participate in co-creating a better work experience!"

While many of the concepts in this book have focused on enterprise strategy and business model choices that are typically made by the CEO and/or senior executives, the reality is that most of the implementation of the Peopletecture ideas is done by front-line leaders, managers, supervisors, and individual contributors. This is where the "rubber meets the road" with respect to translating ideas into reality and helping to make the world of work better for people.

The ability of any organization to know and engage its existing networks, build social capital, avoid silos, and reward collective and individual achievements depends upon the depth and breadth of the implementation of the Peopletecture model. In order to have the maximum benefits of Peopletecture, the launch and cascade of an organization transformation need to be communicated with the entire organization and fully understood by managers and supervisors who can then further reinforce these ideas and put them into action at all levels of an organization.

As you have read in earlier chapters, when senior leaders apply Peopletecture principles, staff feel more supported and thus are more productive, engaged, and committed. They also are more likely to continue working with the organization as it evolves and responds to external and internal changes. And as I wrote earlier, this translates into higher profits and more satisfied customers. It is a rare win-win-win.

So how can managers at all levels make the most of these principles and how should they enact the principles? Once the C-suite has finalized its reorganization strategy, clarified its utility, defined the lines of authority, and communicated this to the organization as a whole and to top-line managers in particular, these managers can take the following key steps to bring all staff on board with the new organizational structure and principles.

Communicate and Engage at All Levels

Communicate, communicate, communicate. I once heard that the only job in leading a team was to have a vision and to articulate it over and over again. In times of transformation, this becomes even

more important. Great management starts with great communication, and part of that is ensuring that everyone understands the
organization's purpose and how the redesign will better deliver on
the company's promise to their customers and their people. These
concepts should not only be told once or sent out in a PowerPoint
or email; they should be reinforced frequently in multiple formats
so that everyone is looking to the same North Star and working
toward the same goals. This is true at the organizational level as
well as at the team level. Your team has its unique purpose and utility within the larger organization.

To start, new or changed jobs and lines of authority should be
communicated with leaders first, and then cascaded to all staff, ideally
with organization charts for quick reference. Typically, the big, macro
decision on moving from one organization model to another happens
with only a small group of people. As such, engaging a broader group
of leaders to describe why and then how the decisions were made
leads to a much higher level of commitment to the new design.

We often approach this part of the transformation by showing
managers and their teams the design principles explored and what
criteria ultimately led to the decisions on the new model. (See Design
Principles Approach in the appendix for additional information on
how to approach this.)

Co-Create Roles and Relationships

However, given that the hierarchy reflected in org charts accounts for
only a small portion of the overall design, it is critical to create and
communicate clear responsibilities and roles at all levels. Applying the
Peopletecture Model, many of the department or division teams
should be heavily involved in consultations to reassess jobs and
responsibilities given the new structure.

When redefining jobs and responsibilities, it is helpful to engage
the people who are doing the work directly impacted by a redesign,
as they will have a sense of what is realistic and possible, as well as
what their capacities, deadlines, and collaborations are. As noted in

Chapter 11, the best outcomes are achieved when teams are empowered to redesign their own work by consciously building interdependencies among teams. Leaders set boundaries for alignment across the organization and teams using network science to inform the optimal connections between teams and help to manage both the emotional and political aspects of change. We have included a Role Crafting Template (see Appendix) that can be used with all individuals and teams to help with this step.

Support Autonomy Consistent with Your Decision-Making Model

For this to work, subordinates must be granted the authority they require to complete a task—that is, the power to make the necessary decisions. In addition, they will need sufficient resources. As noted in Chapter 9, it is about the power and effectiveness of people working together through connection and collaboration, taking responsibility individually and collectively, rather than relying on traditional hierarchical status.

It is critical to your team's cohesion, creativity, and success to ensure all decisions that are made align both with the more specific purpose and utility of your team as well as with the broader purpose and utility of your department/division and the even broader purpose and utility of the organization as a whole. This clarity of focus will help your people feel engaged and help create a more stable team. We have included a tool in the appendix to help you build an accountable team (see Accountable and Empowered Blueprint), which can be used at all levels of the organization to co-create the new design.

Key to this exercise is clarifying the roles and responsibilities of all decision-making participants. This is once again more than simply delegating decision-making authority for the majority of decisions. It ensures that the reports in all levels of the hierarchy have clear accountability for their position in the vertical structure. By doing this, your team(s) can efficiently and effectively enter into workflow relationships with teams and staff outside of your division and hold each other responsible.

Here is another chance to review the concept of the authority ladder. And remember, subordinates must be granted the authority and sufficient resources to make the necessary decisions, and leaders must avoid the tendency to jump in and course-correct once they have empowered their teams to make decisions. When people have the decision-making power and the resources to work toward a meaningful purpose, they are engaged.

Know Your Networks to Connect Silos

All managers benefit from knowing the networks within their division or department. By learning who the Gatekeepers, Pulsetakers, and Hubs are, managers can better facilitate meaningful connections, both broad and deep, between individuals and groups. This will in turn help the sharing of best practices, spark innovation and discovery, and foster effective and meaningful collaborations.

By identifying and engaging your different types of influencers in the network, you can reach and influence the vast majority of the people in your team and division. Understanding the network you are in and who can effect change most effectively is a powerful tool for everyone—be they an individual contributor, team leader, department head, or executive.

As we saw earlier in Chapters 2 and 4, silos have a place in organizations. However, you want to avoid silos that bring specific people together and become a trap and an impediment to communication, collaboration, efficiencies, and innovation. Taking the time to assess why previous silos were so entrenched and debilitating can help your division/department avoid the same mistake again. Using your view of the network can quickly tell you where these silos are hindering your performance. By defining the issues, you can also take concrete steps to address the mistrust, miscommunication, or unnecessary duplication of roles and responsibilities that might have developed over time. Here is another opportunity to bridge your social capital and engage your network.

Context often impacts how we feel about our coworkers. As in my example at the beginning of the chapter, it is likely that Tatiana does not like working with Sarah because they worked in groups that competed with each other in the past. However, now that they will be working together, they are more likely to find common ground and enjoy collaborating. A discussion with both Tatiana and Sarah might also uncover other issues related to previous siloing that may be addressed through the reorganization or, if not, can now be addressed head-on.

Once you know your networks, you can help bridge the social capital. This can be done through a variety of traditional and nontraditional methods:

- Organizing forums
- Designing or adjusting office spaces to foster informal interactions
- Creating inter-functional teams
- Job rotation, temporary and/or permanent work groups
- Having more informal meetings where people may feel freer to share ideas or experiences
- Having a rotating coffee break so that once a month a different department/division hosts and informally shares their work and insights as well as tasty treats
- Regularly sharing team members' presentations/findings/ interviews so others within the team or division can better see how they could collaborate or better leverage their own expertise and insights

Establish and Work Toward (Achievable) Shared Goals Rather Than Individual Performance

As we saw in Chapter 7, shared goals are a powerful motivator for collective action. Setting achievable goals can help to quickly reinforce a sense of common purpose, solidarity, and trust. These goals can be set through a top-down approach (e.g., the organization wants to meet a specific target and thus your division needs to do x by y date) or bottom-up approach (e.g., your team wants to outperform its prior-year performance).

These shared goals can also be the quantitative and qualitative basis for tracking your team's or division's progress or achievements. As such, they also help managers to collectively acknowledge and celebrate a team's or division's progress or achievements. In my client example, they had historically managed their business through a geographic view of profit and loss. This had created strong silos by location, despite the fact that customers didn't buy based on where the broker was located but rather based on their deep expertise in the product or solution. By changing the structure of the hierarchy and network, we addressed some of this. And to reinforce this design, they moved to a single profit-and-loss statement for the entire business. Each new business unit was responsible for its operating margin, but the executives were more heavily goaled and bonused on the corporate performance overall and secondarily on the performance of their unique business.

This shared goaling cascaded to all the teams as well. Managers and their teams were first measured and rewarded on their team's performance and on the performance of the enterprise. The performance management system lined up to reinforce collaborative behaviors that improved team performance. Leaders and managers were also empowered with their own discretionary budgets to reward individual performance using spot awards and quarterly bonuses when they saw an individual going above and beyond to help the team.

Effective communication and collaboration should be acknowledged and rewarded. This will help your team feel more empowered and connected. Team-based rewards foster collaborative focus, which in turn fosters high performers, helping managers better fine-tune their team's responsibilities and results. It bears repeating that research shows that companies with collaborative goals outperform the market 5.5 times. (See the appendix for the Teaming Agreement that can be used to facilitate this dialogue.)

It is also important to acknowledge individual milestones or breakthroughs by celebrating their gaining of new skills, deepening existing skill sets, gaining experience that will help their career, reaching personal work goals, or leading or supporting a key innovation or organizational achievement.

As we explored in Chapter 7, acknowledging and rewarding achievements frequently is a more effective way to increase good work rather than an annual review. It also boosts individual and team morale and commitment. If your organization does not yet permit the distribution of bonuses or other rewards on an ongoing basis, consider recommending they read this book! Or at a minimum, provide them the research that shows the benefits of doing so.

Leaders who use Peopletecture concepts design their organizational context around humans and uphold the purpose and value of the system. They also outperform those that don't. Thus, getting the Peopletecture right is a critical business imperative. Knowing this, where should you start?

13 | Where Should You Start?

"Organizing is what you do before you do something, so that when you do it, it is not all mixed up."

—A.A. Milne

I am obsessed with HGTV. For those not familiar, this is an entire TV network dedicated to watching others shop for, design, renovate, and sell homes. I allow myself to watch it only when on the treadmill or during takeoff and landing on the plane before you are allowed to get your laptop out and start working.

I particularly love the renovation shows. The hosts walk through a dark, messy, overcrowded space and reimagine it with their modern design apps on their tablets, showing the owners (and the viewers) their amazing visions. Then they dismantle the place and rebuild it into a perfect future. We viewers have all laughed at what seemed like a good idea at the time—the 1960s wet bar in the front hall, the 1970s lava rock fireplace, the 1980s roosters on kitchen tiles, and the 1990s giant fiberglass bathtubs.

But in the end, everything is so perfect, organized, clean, and bright that the owners cry at the transformation. In the closing scene, you see them all living happily ever after with friends and family enjoying wine and cheese in the new kitchen or kids and parents going down the slide into their new pool in their resort-style backyards.

There is something incredibly appealing to me (and to many others, it seems, given the success of the network) about rebuilding a space to make it more suitable for the life we live today. Open rooms, storage, outdoor spaces that feel like indoor spaces—these are some of the features buyers and homeowners desire today.

What is notable to me about these shows is the renovators focus on the whole house. These shows never knock down the entire house and start again. They make sure the foundation is sound, the house is safe from electrical issues and roof leaks, and the inside and the outside are both given attention. The owners love the "bones" of their house; they just prefer it to fit the way they currently live and work.

Usually, there is some drama during the renovation, and something has to give: one of the bathrooms doesn't get redone, or the owners have to save the backyard renovation for another time when they have saved up more funds.

One thing they never do is renovate one room at the expense of another. If the plumbing needs to be fixed, they don't put in a new bathroom and then say, "Sorry, now the sink in the kitchen will drip forever," or "You can use the oven, but it will fill the house with smoke." Even if every room doesn't get the perfect makeover, the whole house functions as intended, and the nuts and bolts of the structure work together to make it more livable.

Unlike these fantasy makeovers, business leaders, human resource practitioners, and consultants in organization design often just work on the equivalent of one room to the detriment of the rest of the house. They change one area, one location or something else, and this disrupts how the other areas function.

In many ways, I see myself as one of these passionate renovators. When I go into organizations, there are almost always great features already in place. A solid foundation with lots of possibilities for renovation to move into the twenty-first century is common. To design the ideal renovation for an organization, we cannot just dabble with the separate parts; we must ensure the whole thing functions as intended. Even if it is not as pretty as we hoped, it still works the way we need it to.

Deploy Design Thinking

In his book *The Psychology of Everyday Things*, cognitive scientist and usability engineer Don Norman (2013) describes how even the smartest among us can feel inept when we fail to figure out which light switch or oven burner to turn on or whether to push, pull, or slide a door. He argues the fault lies not with us but with designs that ignore users and the principles of psychology. The problems range from ambiguous and hidden controls to arbitrary relationships between controls and functions, coupled with a lack of feedback or other assistance and unreasonable demands on cognition.

However, good design is possible. The rules are simple: Make things visible, exploit natural relationships that couple function and control, and make intelligent use of constraints. The goal: Guide the individual effortlessly to the right action at the right time.

Originally published in 1988, Norman republished the book with a revised title, *The Design of Everyday Things*, in 2013, citing a better description as the reason. This came at a time when design thinking, an approach that has been slowly evolving since the 1960s, had gained momentum in the business world. In the early stages of design thinking, the profession called on social sciences like psychology and sociology to help practitioners understand how people reacted to new and different ways of doing things.

As Bill Moggridge, British designer, author, and cofounder of the design company IDEO, once said, "I don't think that anyone has really told [people] what design is. It doesn't occur to most people that everything is designed—that every building and everything they touch in the world is designed. Even foods are designed now. So in the process of helping people understand this, making them more aware of the fact that the world around us is something that somebody has control of, perhaps they can feel some sense of control, too. I think that's a nice ambition" (Szczepanska 2017).

In a fun application of design thinking, *Designing Your Life* describes a step-by-step approach to building a joyful life. "What about Purpose?" and "Choosing Happiness" are two of the chapter headings that jumped out to me (Burnett and Evans 2014).

Why not approach the design of an organization in the same way design thinkers approach the design of products and customer experiences? In design thinking, you start with understanding the users (the customers and members of the organization) and design an environment based on their inherent needs and perceptions that they can be successful in.

A New Way to Design Organizations

Truth be told, the basic concepts in the Peopletecture model are not new. Many of the giants that founded the industrial/organizational field studied these same six elements. As an example, Rensis Likert's Four Factor Theory of Leadership contains many of the same concepts—but because he didn't have the computing power we do today, his theory was just a theory. Someone once said that things do not become socially interesting until they become technically boring. With the evolution of computational power, we have the ability to take the organizational psychology theory and use data and analytics from network science to transform how we humans experience work.

Now we know how to use psychology, network science, and design thinking to put the social nature of humans at the center of our organizations. The next phase in this evolution will be to progress our mainstream human resource software packages to hold relational data, not just hierarchal data. This will make it easier and easier to deploy the Peopletecture model. To summarize, deploying the Peopletecture model allows you as the designer to do the following:

1. Build the best hierarchy you can.
2. Create jobs with clarity of ownership based on this hierarchy.
3. Intentionally structure collaboration in the network so that attention is focused in the optimal direction.
4. Remove the organizational scar tissue by putting the right measures for pay and performance in place.
5. Reduce or eliminate the us-versus-them mentality by simplifying and clarifying a person's place of belonging.
6. Provide radical transparency and empower teams.
7. Improve social connections by teaming in ways that make groups wiser.

Who Should Be Doing All This Architecting?

The first two elements of the model, purpose of enterprise and arrangement of valued capabilities, will typically be done at a company's inception by the founder(s) or as ongoing concern by the CEO and executive team, with input from the board and other enterprise leaders. Once these foundational choices are made (not to say they won't be revisited), the architecture of the organization should be turned over to, well, the architects.

Let's go back to our house design analogy. First, decide how you are going to approach the matter of the building's purpose. Will you construct a new building? Buy one? Rent one? Share one with others? Enter into a co-op? Second, decide what value you need to derive to best fit your purpose. Apartment? Townhome? Duplex?

Single-family home? How many rooms do you need? What will be the general purpose of each room? Third, hire an architect, an engineer, and some contractors.

Throughout the book I have laid out the basic principles and key initial questions that must be addressed to design the right model for your business objectives. However, often you will benefit from working with others to delve into your organization and develop a Peopletecture Model. Just as you would not typically undertake the design of a new construction project alone (unless you are a general contractor), so too you should not redesign your organization alone. You should engage experts, either internal or external, in the field of organization design. The complexity of architecting and engineering a stable foundation that can withstand the types of environmental pressures in your specific geography (earthquakes, floods, etc.), coupled with the latest techniques and trends in architecture and design, would often lead you to hire a team of experts.

Your architect works side-by-side with you to design your dream home and so does the organizational designer. If you have ever built a house or done a remodel, you will know that the architect is only one of the key players in getting the house built. Engineers, general contractors, and subcontractors all need to play their part in getting your dream house built.

How to Build an Organization Design Capability

In recent years, building an organization design capability has been a central focus of large enterprises and consulting firms alike. As the business world comes to appreciate that structuring connections is not just an afterthought or a magical art but an actual science that can be measured and, therefore, predicted, the discipline and rigor of design efforts must be facilitated with the right expertise.

When thinking about the types of roles typical in an organization design process, we can continue to lean on our house analogy. In construction, the duties of architects include consulting with clients, sketching designs, and negotiating with other stakeholders. They need to have a combination of architectural expertise and communication skills to consult with clients successfully. This is analogous to the organization design role, which, in the home building sense, is the equivalent of both an architect and engineer. This resource must have an understanding of the business model landscape and deep expertise in how to architect an organization based on science, data, and experience of what works and why.

Where do you find such deep experts in architecting organizations? There are three common places to look. One is internal to your own organization. Perhaps there is an Organization Design Center of Excellence, either as part of the human resources (HR) function or as part of the transformation or strategy function. Or perhaps there are experts in a process improvement area of the business who can be called upon.

The second place to look is in academia. Many deep experts in the different aspects of the Peopletecture model do compelling research demonstrating how humans in groups behave under different organizational conditions, and many of them consult to companies as part of their research.

Finally, and perhaps the most commonplace option today, you can engage a third-party consulting firm. Small boutique firms specialize in parts or all of the Peopletecture dimensions, and some large consulting firms have hundreds and hundreds of organization design specialists who work in different functions and industries.

Regardless of where you find the talent, the most important consideration is having someone who understands how systems work, how tinkering with different parts of the system might impact the whole, and has both the scientific understanding and the business experience to facilitate the right design for your organization.

The next aspect is the role of the HR professional. Their job can really be paralleled to that of a general contractor because they oversee all aspects of a project. A general contractor's main duties include engaging with subcontractors and providing hands-on guidance to workers on the site. Our HR partners in business today connect the organization design experts with the company's HR practices and the business leaders driving the decisions on how to configure the six aspects of the Peopletecture Model.

The business leader roles can be equated to the owner of the property being designed and built—"the client." The back office or center leader role can be equated to a subcontractor. Subcontractors receive work from general contractors and perform part of the labor of the project. They focus on using their unique/specialized skill set to benefit a project. These three types of roles work together in concert to architect and implement the new design.

14 | Conclusion: What's Next?

"Any company designed for success in the twentieth century is doomed to failure in the twenty-first."
—David Rose, angel investor

Now, I may be a glass-half-full person, but this is the most exciting time to be an organization designer in the history of work. I wrote this book during the global COVID-19 pandemic. During this two-year period, the importance and value of network insights were brought to the forefront of business.

Let me answer the most oft-asked question in business at this moment: "When do we really need to be at work in-person?" Let's assume we end up with a two-days-a-week-in-the-office arrangement. While there is no "one size fits all" or silver bullet to optimize a hybrid workforce, it's critical that we make these face-time collaboration opportunities count. Outside of the known benefits to engagement, innovation, and performance from informal interactions at lunch, around the water cooler, and after-work socializing, what intentional collaboration must we facilitate to make in-office time worth it for both employees and employers?

We live and breathe in a tsunami of interconnections. We need to understand the nature of connections so we can change and improve them. Prior to the dramatic shift to virtual work, we used to discuss the networks built based on where you sat in your office. Researchers repeatedly demonstrated that if you sat more than 30 feet from a coworker, you were unlikely to have much of a connection (Morgan 2012).

Traditional office space was created a couple hundred years ago, when information was not mobilized. Because so much information is no longer geographically bound, we are no longer tethered to the office. We should reinvent the concept of office space and how we use it to collaborate. We need to take advantage of this inflection point in the history of work and change the way we use proximity for work. But how?

To best answer this, we can look at two evidence-based phenomena that we discussed in this book. One is social capital, which can be measured and visualized with network science. Some have called visualizing these relationships the "traces of trust." The second is collective intelligence. Once we understand the network changes that have occurred from 2020 to 2022 in relation to these two important factors in business performance, we can bring back Peopletecture principles to craft return-to-office strategies and plans that will increase engagement and growth and decrease burnout and turnover.

Improving Social Capital

To understand how to improve social capital, we need only look at the types of collaboration that benefited in a 100% remote working environment during the 2020–2022 pandemic period and those that did not.

When shocks occur, organizational networks tend *not* to display structural changes associated with adaptiveness. Rather, the network "turtles." In layperson's terms, think of a turtle on its back. The turtle thinks it's fine and does not understand that its demise is imminent.

In network science terms, the organization displays a propensity for higher clustering, strong tie interaction, and an intensification of insider-versus-outsider communication. Instead of activating loose ties to get novel information needed to adapt to a changing environment, we double-down on our close ties and spend time connecting with those most like us.

We turtle because of our human nature. (Recall homophily and the other evolutionarily based reasons described earlier in the book.) While strong evidence suggests that networks facing shocks turtle up rather than open up, some findings indicate that networks are relatively elastic—turtled-up states return to normal states relatively fast. However, this return to the "normal" in-office-five-days-a-week scenario will likely never be the norm again. Moreover, recent data shows that the loose ties that diminished or disappeared during 2020–2022 have not returned to their former state; instead, they remain permanently diminished a significant amount (Yang et al., 2022).

We have seen that strong ties strengthened during pandemic, and weak ties weakened. This is a problem for organizations and for the people who work in them. Network scientist Ronald Burt has long demonstrated the fragility of bridging connections, showing a 90% decay within a year if there is no intentional purpose to keeping them active (Burt 2001). After all, it takes energy to form and maintain a relationship, but it takes no energy to let one disappear. And with virtual work, there is about a 30% decay of bridge connections—permanently (Burt 2001).

Bridging connections can and should be driven by purpose (e.g., what we're trying to achieve together). Over the pandemic period, some groups increased bridging connections virtually because teams and companies were very intentional about cross-functional teaming around strategies and missions and intentionally structured these ties. But left to chance, bridging connections will erode.

In our virtual work data, we can see relationships within the network favoring strong ties, high clustering, and company insiders. But what of the new joiners during the pandemic or those who did not have a strong network before we went fully virtual? We can also use social capital metrics to understand exactly who is at risk of quitting due to burnout and who is at risk of quitting due to isolation. And knowing this, we can intentionally connect those high-talent individuals using proximity to accelerate connectivity and trust.

Traces of Trust

We know that we need to create rigor and routines intentionally to bridge connections, and we know it takes a lot more effort to do this virtually. In face-to-face interactions, it takes about five to six interactions to build social capital in which we have a strong trust tie. In virtual interactions, it takes 15 to 18 interactions (i.e., more intention) to get to that same point (Cross 2021).

Just think of the implications of this, because it's not just more collaboration that is the challenge. If it takes three times the number of interactions to build trust and social capital, then you need to decrease the number of people you are bridging with by one-third. And this doesn't even address influencing someone to adopt a new idea. As much as 80% of our ability to influence someone is in person, eyeball to eyeball (Cross 2021).

Certainly, current return-to-office policies acknowledge the benefits of face-to-face interactions, but few companies use data and science with intention in the way they could be. Commonly, people come back to the office, and their teammates are not there, or another team that someone might want to build a bridge with is not there, so those people don't get the benefit of proximity for social capital.

Organizations that have been using technology for virtual collaboration have at least two years of network data at their fingertips. All the meetings and messages that we shared between our coworkers are digital traces of relationships. For almost every organization around the globe, the possibility of leveraging their own network data and insights to inform a new world of work is profound. Those companies that are starting to take advantage of these incredible insights are able to understand their organizations in an entirely new way.

For example, at a large technology company, their data revealed that the shift to virtual work created a decrease in loose ties between different functions in the organization, most likely due to the lack of face-to-face interactions. They knew that these relationships were linked to innovation, creativity, and knowledge sharing (Wu et al. 2008) and that they had to get them back. Thus, they set about implementing return-to-office strategies using collaboration spaces and structured meetings to intentionally increase the interaction between these different resources (Wu et al. 2008). They are already starting to see an increase in their loose-tie relationships in their data.

Networks are not random, as science shows. If you can understand a network, you can change the way it acts. You *cannot legislate trust*, but you can create conditions for trust to grow in a healthy environment. Virtual work exacerbates tribalism or in-group/out-group behaviors. We need time together to overcome this.

Collective Intelligence

Albert Einstein famously said that a problem couldn't be solved with the same level of consciousness that created it in the first place. It astounds me that we have known for a long time that collective intelligence (CI) diminishes when we use video as a communication medium on a team, yet this has been a prominent collaboration tool, especially since the start of the pandemic.

As a refresher, CI is the ability of a group to solve a wide range of problems. Evidence of this general collective intelligence factor explains a group's performance on a wide variety of tasks. This CI factor is not strongly correlated with the average or maximum individual intelligence of group members but is correlated with the average social sensitivity of group members and the equality in distribution of conversational turn taking (Wooley et al. 2010).

Studies conducted prior to the COVID-19 pandemic hypothesized and tested the effect of nonverbal synchrony on CI that develops through visual and audio cues in physically separated teammates. They showed that, contrary to popular belief, the presence of visual cues surprisingly has no effect on CI. Furthermore, teams without visual cues are more successful in synchronizing their vocal cues and speaking turns, and when they do so, they have higher CI (Wooley et al. 2010).

These findings show that nonverbal synchrony is important in distributed collaboration and call into question the necessity of video support (Tomprou et al. 2021). The study underscores the importance of audio cues, which appear to be compromised by video access.

Before March 2020, most of us were in the office most days, and when we were not, we worked virtually. This was mostly via telephone. We called into meetings during our commute, when we were traveling for work, and when we were working from home. Sure, we used video conferences on occasion—global meetings where international travel was impractical, team meetings where groups were in different locations, or, for some of the more progressive companies, recurring standing meetings or "all-hands" webcasts.

Starting in spring 2020, however, virtually all meetings suddenly went to video. This included the ones we used to do in-person, the ones we used to do on the phone, and the ones we were already doing via video. For the first few weeks, it was interesting. We enjoyed the random kids and pets joining our work meetings, often at inopportune times. We said, "This is making work more human!"

But after this 24-month experiment, we saw and heard a tidal wave of complaints. As one TikToker lamented during her company's "mental health" week, "It's okay not to be okay, as long as you are still contactable at all times via email!" Despite our video connectivity, we had a second pandemic of social isolation.

Social isolation is one of the strongest predictors of physical health problems, and intuitively, we know it is what is causing burnout in the workplace. The World Health Organization (2019) defines burnout as "a syndrome conceptualized as resulting from chronic workplace stress that has not been successfully managed." In network analysis, we see that people who are high on work network (overloaded with work and collaboration demands) but low on social network (isolated from friends, mentors, and sponsors) are suffering from burnout.

Other findings point to a shift in collaboration. The time employees had previously spent interacting face-to-face with their core teams and managers was replaced with less-rich forms of interaction, such as email and large group video meetings. This decline was due to the weakening of social connections with close peers and management, which contribute to employees' ability to gather the context they need to meet deadlines and ensure they focus on the right work.

Instead of interacting in-person, they compensated with emails, which are less effective for developing social connections and communicating complex ideas. Additionally, employees were struggling to balance finding time for meaningful interactions, while also focusing on getting their work done within an 8-hour work day. By the end of this 24-month period, employees were working on average 3 more hours per day (Humanyze 2022).

My colleague Jeff Schwartz, who recently wrote a great book on the future of work called *Work Disrupted* (2021), used to talk about the three elements of work, workforce, and workplace and how these elements will change organizations as we know them over time. I think we all believed, prior to the pandemic, that it would be the automation of work and the continued rise of the gig economy that would be the driver of these changes. We could never have predicted it would be the workplace that would actually become the catalyst for transformation of the organization.

What is fascinating about this driver is the connection to network analytics and our ability to understand the benefits of co-location of teams based on the type of work and the type of worker. Co-location of a highly educated population is a not-so-secret secret of Silicon Valley. Thirteen percent of people living in Palo Alto hold a PhD. Success comes from the flow of ideas. Beyond information flows, there is an even stronger symbiosis that drives both the high-tech companies and the highly skilled workers to locate in the same place (Jackson 2019).

Proximity has a huge influence on our relationships. In its most recent workforce survey, Gallup found that just 17% of hybrid workers reported having a best friend at work, the lowest level that it's ever been in the many decades it has been conducting its engagement studies (*New York Times* 2022). For those who don't have friends at work, work can feel lonely and lead to disengagement and turnover. People on the periphery of a network are 60% more likely to leave.

In fact, using network data to study virtual collaboration patterns over the two years of the global COVID-19 pandemic reveals a great deal of insights on how work is getting done. For example, we can study loose collaboration patterns that used to take place in the office to see what happened when everyone started to work virtually. Loose collaborators are colleagues an employee interacts with for less than an hour or two per week on average. These types of connections tend to rely heavily on informal interactions around the office and therefore may be significantly impacted with a fully remote workforce. Research shows that these informal communication styles and structures are vital for innovation, creativity, and knowledge-sharing across an organization.

One company studied collaboration after returning to the office to determine best use of office space. The company was able to implement strategic resourcing, program, and proximity decisions to help key groups come together. It also used the collaboration pattern data to relocate functions that needed more interaction with the rest of the organization. With objective insights on how, where, and with whom teams worked, the company was able to make cross-functional project deliveries more efficient and increase opportunities for internal networking and innovation.

As we start to implement our "hybrid return-to-office" strategies, many employee perception surveys show that employees wish to spend the majority of their work week remotely, with a minority of their work time in the office (Fealy and Feinsod 2022). As companies decide how to make work for all their people, what will become of the 10-hour-day video meeting?

Let's apply the Peopletecture Model to answer this question. The *hierarchical* structures in organizations create a frame for our experiences at work. We have strong ties within our hierarchy, and in this frame, we become *members* of a group where we feel a sense of belonging. These ties can continue to be nurtured primarily virtually because we have consistent interaction and high degrees of trust.

But we must also *team* effectively within and between social *networks* to get the full benefit of being part of an organization. For building and expanding on these types of network relationships, we need to step away from the video conference, get dressed, drive into the office, and make in-person connections. In either model, we need to empower people to take *responsibility* for their part of the work that needs to be done. And we need our management system to fairly measure and reward those who work virtually, in-person, or in some hybrid of the two.

The Workplace of the Future

Today we are planning for two uses for the office of the future: event space and collaboration space. Let us first examine the power of event space. Humans at times have a hive-ish nature. In fact, social psychologist Jonathan Haidt says that we are 10% bee (2012). If we activate the hive switch, we see incredible leaps in trust, a sense of community, and a higher purpose. How do we activate the hive switch at work?

Use events to bridge the bonding gap. When we look at neuroimaging, we see events such as chanting or humming, dancing together, eating and drinking, emotional storytelling, and laughter all trigger the endorphin system and increase the sense of belonging (Dunbar 2022).

With respect to collaboration space, form follows function. We need to ponder what social form is necessary to best accomplish that intent. Innovation, growth, and new ideas require a different configuration for collaboration than routine tasks that are predictable, efficient, and productive. If you had only one rule of thumb, make it this: If the work is simple and explicit, do it virtually. If it's complex and tacit, do it using proximity because this will accelerate the business outcome you are trying to achieve.

When it comes to directing teams for collaboration in-person versus virtually, think about the stage the team is at. Perhaps create a discover-build-scale framework, as each requires different network configurations. Choose some sort of recipe for proximity. As an example, at the front end of a project, interacting with diverse groups for new ideas requires bridging connections, so set up meetings with different teams in-person. Start with what you are trying to solve for and be intentional, then think about when to come in and with whom. Another way to think about it is "heads-up" and "heads-down" work. Virtual work is more produc-tive for heads-down work because you don't have shifting costs of meetings, interruptions, etc.

The old way of understanding our collective behaviors was by looking at the choices of individuals. A better understanding of social networks is essential for facing the challenges in our new world of work. The six elements of Peopletecture—hierarchy, networks, measurements, membership, teaming, and responsibility—are wired into our brains. They developed over the history of our species to address adaptive challenges. As I write, we are facing our next challenge in the world of work: Knowledge workers are beginning to return to the office. Data trends have shifted over the past year with respect to employee preference between virtual and in-office, with the current data showing an average preference of two to three days at a designated work location and the rest remote and flexible.

None of us knows for certain what the future of work will look like, but we now have both the research and real-world understanding of all six elements of Peopletecture and how they operate in concert to address adaptive challenges. By linking the study of individual behavior to the study of group dynamics using network science, we can finally explain much of our behavior at work. Thus, there is not a timelier use of Peopletecture insights to help us craft an adaptive workplace. Instead of trying to anticipate the future, let's create it.

Appendix

Design Principles Approach

Developing design principles

- Design principles set the strategic guidelines for the organizational design.
- Design principles establish and maintain good design practice, ensure consistency and guide the design against aligned criteria.

Example design principles

Customer intimacy:
Drive high levels of customer retention through a centralized strong service support network.

Accountability:
Optimize spans of control to speed decision-making and enhance individual accountability.

Cost optimization:
Efficiently manage costs by capitalizing on desired factors and reducing undesired ones.

Innovation:
Drive focus of new products and efficiency.

Agility and scalability:
A flexible model and structure allows for addition of any new products/services and response time to market.

Aligning principles with testable design criteria

What are design criteria?
- A way to test and weigh the trade-offs and considerations among different design alternatives
- Objective and easy to assess
- Applied for each design principle that you plan to use to evaluate your design with

Example design principle	Example design criteria
Customer Intimacy	Focused, dedicated resources aligned to customer groups or customer journey
Cost Optimization	Minimizes coordination (or "middleperson") roles whose primary responsibility is to liaise between two groups
Accountability	Optimal span of control (5–8) to speed decision-making and enhance individual accountability
Agility and Scalability	Creates pools of teams to respond quickly to changing business needs

Note: the amount and type of design principles will vary by project

Role Crafting Template

Job design versus role crafting

So why not just focus on writing **job descriptions** or **role profiles**?
- Job descriptions clarify what a job is (largely in isolation), designed to accomplish tasks for the organization.
- Role crafting is about clarity on how an individual can deliver on a role, designed to maximize outcomes for the organization.

> **I do these things for my job**
>
> **versus**
>
> **I deliver on these experiences for my role**

What is role crafting?

What is role crafting?

- Role crafting is a method for actively designing your role on each of the teams you are on that best suits your strengths and passions.
- This effort is proven to lead to greater enjoyment, meaning, and effectiveness at work, and as a result higher team performance, and is based on cutting-edge academic research.
- It encourages you to think about your role on a team in a new way. Helps you resourcefully use elements in the tasks in your role to make your work more engaging and fulfilling.

What are some benefits of role crafting?

- Designs roles that are best suited to you and your strengths to maximize outcomes.
- Increases meaning and purpose of roles resulting in more productivity.[1]
- Personalizes roles which can dramatically increase engagement and enjoyment with work.

Approach for role crafting

The approach has two parts and takes about 1–2 hours to complete.
- Part A of the approach helps you take a step back and gauge how you want to spend your time based on what is meaningful and what you find strengthening.
- Part B helps you identify opportunities to craft an ideal—but still realistic—version of your role.

Part A	Part B

1. **Before Sketch** (20 minutes): Participants complete their Before Sketches, producing 8–10 tasks they are or anticipate doing, from spending most time to spending least time.
 	
2. **Discussing the Before Sketch** (10 minutes): In the team, participants discuss what the work is and what they each are passionate about and good at.
	1. **After Diagram** (50 minutes): Participants complete their ideal role and list out their main collaboration partners. This step involves grouping your role into three types of Task Blocks. The biggest of these blocks are for tasks that consume the most of your effort, attention, and time; the smallest blocks are for the least energy-, attention-, and time-intensive tasks, and some will fall into the middle, "medium-sized" blocks. Choose aspects of the role that you have been asked to play in ways that
	  • make negative aspects of your assignment better or
	  • expand upon and reinforce the positive aspects of your role.
	  • Can you add, drop, or change aspects of your job to improve your sense of fit?
	  • How can you connect with people who energize you more frequently and adapt your collaboration patterns?
	
	2. **Discussing the After Diagram** (15 minutes): In team or subgroups, participants discuss their After Diagrams. Possible questions to spark discussion: What insights did the exercise reveal? What opportunities for action did the exercise uncover? What challenges do you anticipate in crafting your role and your collaborators? How might you deal with or overcome these challenges?
	
	3. **Action Plan** (15 minutes): Participants complete an Action Plan
	
	4. **Whole group debrief** (5 minutes): Invite the team or small groups to share their insights, comments, or feedback.

Accountable and Empowered Blueprint

The "AE" method: An alternative approach to decision rights and governance

The AE method is a simplified approach to decision rights, used as an alternative to RACI. This method focuses on where decisions are made and where they are delegated:

- **Authority** — Leadership decision to make, where you must do it yourself
- **Empowerment** — Group decision to make, where you empower others

Top-down or bottom-up decision-making

Responsibility will be cultivated in two ways:

- Top-down executive understanding of what decisions will need to be held and which should be given to teams
- Bottom-up teams working horizontally to solve issues

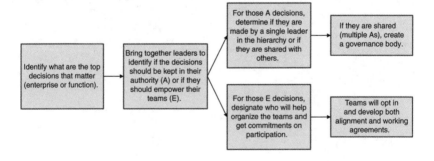

How to define top-down or bottom-up decision-making

Top down

Defining authority and empowerment

- **Authority**: Leadership decision to make, where you must do it yourself; this is about 25% of decisions.

- **Empowerment**: Group decision to make; this is about 75% of decisions.

- **Choose A when** there are high negative or positive consequences to you and your organization. You have significant experience in dealing with these kinds of decisions. Think risk management, ethics, brand, or other critical aspects that need to be consistently and uniformly managed.

- **Choose E when** stakes are high and there is someone more expert that should own the decision. Or you may be the expert, but the consequences are low thus making it a great learning opportunity for another. Or the decision is both not important and not in your wheelhouse and effort on it should be minimized.

Bottom up

Teams focused on scope and working agreements

- Redesign the position control process to minimize the effort needed to get approvals (especially when it is within budget).

- Establish a team charter.

Process to evaluate and define team norms

1. Decision-making and problem solving
2. Uncertainty and conflict management
3. Meetings and communication
4. Accountability and monitoring
5. Additional working norms

1 Review five pillars of team norm agreements

2 Review diagnostic, solutioning, commitment framework

3 Develop and commit to team norms

- Diagnostic: What is working and not working for our team?
- Solutioning: What can we do to improve how our team works together?
- Commitment: What are our agreed team norms?

Step 1: Five pillars inform a team's working norms

Guiding principles	Decision-making and problem solving	How does my team come to conclusions and solutions?
How do the values and behaviors guide our work?	Uncertainty and conflict management	What do we do to manage conflicts and questions across the team?
	Meetings and communication	How do we ensure effective meetings and clear communications?
	Accountability and monitoring	How do we ensure our work is getting done?
	Additional working norms	What other principles guide our work and team practices?

Step 2: Arriving at our team norms

Each of the following will be carried out for all five pillars of team norms:

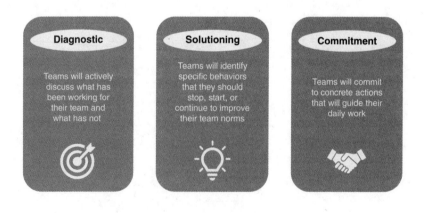

Diagnostic
Teams will actively discuss what has been working for their team and what has not

Solutioning
Teams will identify specific behaviors that they should stop, start, or continue to improve their team norms

Commitment
Teams will commit to concrete actions that will guide their daily work

Step 2a: Diagnostic: How is our team working?

Decision-making and problem solving	**What is working well for our team?**
Uncertainty and conflict management	
Meetings and communication	
Accountability and monitoring	**What is not working for our team?**
Additional working norms	

Step 2b: Solutioning: How will we improve?

	What do we do that we should preserve?	What should we put in place to improve our way of working?	What should we stop doing?
Decision-making and problem solving			
Uncertainty and conflict management			
Meetings and communication			

Step 2b: Solutioning: How will we improve?

	What do we do that we should preserve?	What should we put in place to improve our way of working?	What should we stop doing?
Accountability and monitoring			
Additional working norms			

Step 2c: Commitment: What are we agreeing to?

Considering the values, outline the team's guiding principles below:

Guidance
Fill in this template by outlining which characteristics of the values are most important to the team. Write them to be directly relevant to the team's context.

Examples
"Promote collaboration from within and outside our team on all deliverables, seeking guidance from and respecting the expertise of our cross-team counterparts."

"Keep execution goals in mind at all times, creating team processes that are efficient and effective."

Guiding principles

Step 2c: Commitment: What are we agreeing to?

Keep in mind the team's guiding principles.

Decision-making and problem solving	
Uncertainty and conflict management	
Meetings and communication	
Accountability and monitoring	
Additional working norms	

Step 2c: Commitment: What are our next steps?

Actions we should immediately take to follow through on our committed norms.

Decision-making and problem solving	
Uncertainty and conflict management	
Meetings and communication	
Accountability and monitoring	
Additional working norms	

Step 2c: Commitment: What are our next steps?

- Keep in mind the team's guiding principles.

Decision-making and problem solving	"Explain rationale for decisions to entire team." "Offer solutions, don't just raise issues."
Uncertainty and conflict management	"Address issues as soon as they arise." "Speak to the individual(s) involved before escalating."
Meetings and communication	"Arrive on time to every meeting." "Send important messages or questions over email for quick reference."
Accountability and monitoring	"Weekly check-ins to assess progress on large projects." "In-person meetings to address accountability issues."
Additional working norms	"Work with team to create coverage plans 2+ weeks before vacation." "Use team SharePoint to ensure consistency in shared documents."

Examples

References

Chapter 1

Dignan, A. (2019). *Brave new work: Are you ready to reinvent your organization?* New York: Portfolio/Penguin.

Duhigg, C. (2016). What Google learned from its quest to build the perfect team. *The New York Times Magazine*, 25 February. Available from: https://www.nytimes.com/2016/02/28/magazine/what-google-learned-from-its-quest-to-build-the-perfect-team.html [accessed: 29 August, 2022].

Goran, J., LaBerge, L., and Srinivasan, R. (2017). *Culture for a digital age*. Available from: https://www.mckinsey.com/business-functions/mckinsey-digital/our-insights/culture-for-a-digital-age [accessed 9/11/2022].

Greater Good. (2019). *Greater good: The science of a meaningful life* [online]. Available from: https://greatergood.berkeley.edu/ [accessed 9/11/2022].

Hamel, G. and Zanini, M. (2020). *Humanocracy*. Boston: Harvard Business Review Press.

Kleiner, A. (2002). *Karen Stephenson's quantum theory of trust*. Available from: https://www.strategy-business.com/article/20964 [accessed 29 August 2022].

Minnaar, J. and de Morree, P. (2019). *Corporate rebels: Make work more fun*. New York: Corporate Rebels Nederland BV.

179

Morieux, Y. and Tollman, P. (2014). *Six simple rules: How to manage complexity without getting complicated.* Boston: Harvard Business Review Press.

Robbins, T. (2007). *Awaken the giant within.* New York: Simon & Schuster.

Wigert, B. (2020). *Employee burnout: The biggest myth.* Available from: https://www.gallup.com/workplace/288539/employee-burnout-biggest-myth.aspx. [accessed 11 September 2022].

Chapter 2

Adams, J.S. (2020). *Equity theory: Process of model of motivation.* Available from: https://www.youtube.com/watch?v=ksnCw96-vg7M [accessed 9/11/2022].'

Cross, R. (2021). *Beyond collaboration overload.* Boston: Harvard Business Review Press.

Deming, W.E. (2018). *Out of the crisis.* Cambridge: The MIT Press.

Dignan, A. (2019). *Brave new work: Are you ready to reinvent your organization?* New York: Portfolio/Penguin.

Haidt, J. (2012). *The righteous mind: Why good people are divided by politics and religion.* New York: Vintage Books.

Jaques, E. (1990). In praise of hierarchy. *Harvard Business Review,* 68(1), pp. 127–133.

Laloux, F. (2014). *Reinventing organizations.* Millis MA: Nelson Parker.

Mochari, I. (2014). *The case for hierarchy.* Available from: https://www.inc.com/ilan-mochari/case-for-hierarchy.html [accessed 11 September 2022].

Morieux, Y. (2014). *As work gets more complex, 6 rules to simplify.* Available from: https://www.youtube.com/watch?v=0MD4Y-mjyc2I [accessed 11 September 2022].

Nicholson, N. (1998). How hardwired is human behavior? *HBR Magazine,* July–August.

National Institutes of Health. (2008). *Human brain appears "hard-wired" for hierarchy.* Available from: https://www.nih.gov/news-events/

news-releases/human-brain-appears-hard-wired-hierarchy [accessed 10 September 2022].

Pink, D. (2011). *Drive: The surprising truth about what motivates us.* New York: Riverhead Books.

Weller, C. (2019). *3 big ideas to revolutionize performance conversations.* Available from: https://neuroleadership.com/your-brain-at-work/performance-conversations-3-big-ideas [accessed 11 September 2022].

Chapter 3

Cole, N.L. (2020). *Units of analysis as related to sociology.* Available from: https://www.thoughtco.com/wh-units-of-analysis-matter-4019028 [accessed 11 September 2022].

Meadows, D. (2008). *Thinking in systems: A primer.* White River Junstion, VT: Sustainability Institute, p. 14.

Oshry, B. (2018). *Context, context, context: How our blindness to context cripples even the smartest organizations.* Axminster: Triarchy Press.

Pflaeging, N. (2020). *Organize for complexity.* BetaCodex Publishing, p. 19.

Turchin, P. (2020, December). The next decade could be even worse. *The Atlantic.*

Chapter 4

Culen, J. (2017). *Hierarchy, informal networks and how to navigate the full mess.* Available from: https://juliaculen.medium.com/hierarchy-informal-networks-and-how-to-navigate-the-full-mess-89d442b096a2 [accessed 11 September 2022].

De Smet, A., Kleinman, S., and Weerda, K. (2019). *The helix organization.* Available from: https://www.mckinsey.com/business-functions/people-and-organizational-performance/our-insights/the-helix-organization [accessed 11 September 2022].

FAQs for Organizations. (2016). *Vertical leverage.* Available from: http://www.faqsfororgs.com/vertical-leverage/ [accessed 11 September 2022].

Galbraith, J. (2014). *Designing organizations: Strategy, structure, and process at the business unit and enterprise levels.* San Francisco: Josey-Bass.

Hannan, M.T. and Freeman, J. (1984). Structural inertia and organizational change. *American Sociological Review.*

Hörrmann, G. and Tiby, C. (1990). Project Management made correctly. *Management of the high-performance organization.* Wiesbaden: pp. 73–91. (In German).

Jaques, E. (1990). In praise of hierarchy. *Harvard Business Review*, 68(1), pp. 127–133.

Lencioni, P. (2006). *Silos, politics, and turf wars.* San Francisco: Jossey-Bass.

Levitin, D.J. (2015). *The organized mind: Thinking straight in the age of information overload.* New York: Dutton.

McChrystal, S. (2015). *Team of teams.* New York: Portfolio/Penguin.

Oshry, B. (2018). *Context, context, context: How our blindness to context cripples even the smartest organizations.* Axminster: Triarchy Press.

Shirky, C. (2008). *Here comes everybody: The power of organizing without organizations.* New York: Penguin Books.

Weber, M. (2022). *Chain of command principle.* Available from: https://www.referenceforbusiness.com/management/Bun-Comp/Chain-of-Command-Principle.html [accessed 11 September 2022].

Chapter 5

Arena, M. (2018). *Adaptive space: How GM and other companies are positively disrupting themselves and transforming into agile organizations.* New York: McGraw-Hill Education.

Bhagat, S., Burke, M., and Diuk, C. (2016). *Three and a half degrees of separation.* Available from: https://research.facebook.com/blog/2016/02/three-and-a-half-degrees-of-separation [accessed 11 September 2022].

Brass, D.J. (1984). Being in the right place: A structural analysis of individual influence in an organization. *Administrative Science Quarterly*, 29, pp. 518–539.

Burt, R. (2004). The social origins of good ideas. *American Journal of Sociology.*

Burt, R.S. (1992). *Structural holes: The social structure of competition.* Cambridge, MA: Harvard University Press.

Cross, R. (2021). *Beyond collaboration overload.* Boston: Harvard Business Review Press.

Fass, C., Ginelli, M., and Turtle, B. (1996). *Six degrees of Kevin Bacon.* New York: Plume.

Gladwell, M. (2002). *The tipping point.* New York: Back Bay Books.

Goran, J., LaBerge, L., and Srinivasan, R. (2017) *Culture for a digital age.* Available from: https://www.mckinsey.com/business-functions/mckinsey-digital/our-insights/culture-for-a-digital-age [accessed 11 September 2022].

Jackson, M. (2019). *The human network: How your social position determines your power, beliefs, and behaviors.* New York: Vintage Books.

Krackhardt, D. and Hansen, J. (1993). *Informal networks: The company behind the chart.* Available from: https://hbr.org/1993/07/informal-networks-the-company-behind-the-chart [accessed 13 September 2022].

Krebs, V. (2007). Managing 21st century organizations. *IHRIM Journal*, XI(4).

Lin, N. (2001). *Social capital: A theory of social structure and action.* Cambridge: Cambridge University Press.

McDowell, T. (2016). *Organizational network analysis.* Available from: https://www2.deloitte.com/content/dam/Deloitte/us/Documents/human-capital/us-cons-organizational-network-analysis.pdf [accessed 11 September 2022].

Milgram, S. (1967). The small world problem. *Psychology Today*, 2, pp. 60–67.

Romero, D.M., Uzzi, B., and Kleinberg, J. (2016). Social networks under stress. *Social and Information Networks.*

Shapiro, C. and Varian, H. (1990). *Information rules: A strategic guide to the network economy.* Boston: Harvard Business School Press.

Shirky, C. (2008). *Here comes everybody: The power of organizing without organizations.* New York: Penguin Books.

Stephenson, K. (2005). Trafficking in trust: The DNA of social capital. In L. Coughlin, E. Wingard, and K. Hollihan (Eds.), *Enlightened power: How women are transforming the practice of leadership* (pp. 243–266). San Francisco: Jossey-Bass.

Uzzi, B. (1997). Social structure and competition in interfirm networks: the paradox of embeddedness. *Administrative Science Quarterly.* 42, pp. 35–67.

Chapter 6

King, H. (2020). Flow: The emerging paradigm. *Henry King*, 31 July.

Powell, W.W. (1990). Neither market nor hierarchy: Network forms of organization 12. *Research in Organizational Behaviour,* pp. 295–336.

Soda, G. and Zaheer, A. (2012). A network perspective on organizational architecture: Performance effects of the interplay of formal and informal organization. *Strategic Management Journal.*

Stephenson, K. (2021). Social capital analysis: The newest and strongest tool for driving strategic impact. *NetForm Resources*, November 24.

Chapter 7

Ariely, D. (2013). *What makes us feel good about our work?* Available from: https://www.ted.com/talks/dan_ariely_what_makes_us_feel_good_about_our_work?language=en#t-604603 [accessed 9/13/2022].

Buckingham, M. and Goodall, A. (2019). *Nine lies about work: A freethinking leader's guide to the real world*. Boston: Harvard Business Review Press.

Cable, D. (2019). *Alive at work: The neuroscience of helping your people love what they do*. Boston: Harvard Business Review Press.

Clarridge, T. (2020). Shared goals, shared purpose, shared vision. *Social Capital Research*.

Deming, W.E (1993). *The new economics for industry, government, education*. Cambridge: Massachusetts Institute of Technology Center for Advanced Engineering Study.

Harris, M. and Tayler, B. (2019). Don't let metrics undermine your business. *Harvard Business Review*, September–October.

Kates, A., Kesler, G., and DiMartino, M, (2021). *Networked, scaled, and agile*. London: Kogan Page Ltd.

Kerr, S. (1995). On the folly of rewarding A while hoping for B. *The Academy of Management Executive, 9*.

King, H. (2020). Flow: The emerging paradigm. *Henry King, 31 July*.

Kohn, A. (2018). *Punished by rewards: Twenty-fifth anniversary edition: The trouble with gold stars, incentive plans, A's, praise, and other bribes*. Boston: Mariner Books.

Morieux, Y. and Tollman, P. (2014). *Six simple rules: How to manage complexity without getting complicated*. Boston: Harvard Business Review Press.

O'Boyle, E. and Aguinis, A. (2012). The best and the rest: Revisiting the norm of normality of individual performance. *Personnel Psychology*.

Pink, D. (2011). *Drive: The surprising truth about what motivates us*. New York: Riverhead Books.

Podolny, J.M. and Hansen, M.T. (2020). How Apple is organized for innovation. It's about experts leading experts. *HBR Magazine*, November–December.

Schwartz, J. et al. (2020). The compensation conundrum. *Deloitte, 15 May*.

Townsend, R.C. and Bennis, W. (2007). *Up the organization: How to stop the corporation from stifling people and strangling profits*. New York: John Wiley & Sons.

Chapter 8

Adler, P.S. and Kwon, S-W. (2002). Social capital: Prospects for a new concept. *The Academy of Management Review* 27(1), pp. 17–40.

Baumeister, R. and Leary, M. (1995). The need to belong: Desire for interpersonal attachments as a fundamental human motivation. *Psychological Bulletin*, p. 497.

Berg, J.M., Dutton, J.E., and Wrzesniewski, A. (2001). Job crafting and meaningful work. *American Psychological Association*.

BetterUp. (2021). The value of belonging at work: New frontiers for inclusion in 2021 and beyond. Available from: https://grow.betterup.com/resources/the-value-of-belonging-at-work-the-business-case-for-investing-in-workplace-inclusion [accessed 12 September 2022].

Bregman, R. (2020). *Humankind: A hopeful history*. New York: Little, Brown and Company.

Chow, W. S. and Chan, L. S. (2008). Social network, social trust and shared goals in organizational knowledge sharing. *Information & Management*, 45(7), pp. 458–465.

Claridge, T. (2004). *Social capital and natural resource management*. Unpublished Thesis.

Darwin, C. (1871). *The descent of man and selection in relation to sex*. Amherst NY: Prometheus Books.

Edmondson, A. and Harvey, J-F. (2017). *Extreme teaming. Lessons in complex, cross-sector leadership*. Bingley: Emerald Publishing.

Haidt, J. (2012). *The righteous mind: Why good people are divided by politics and religion*. New York: Vintage Books.

Hare, B. and Woods, V. (2020). *Survival of the friendliest: Understanding our origins and rediscovering our common humanity*. New York: Random House.

Islam, G. (2014). Social identity theory. *Encyclopedia of Critical Psychology*. New York: Springer.

Leana, C., Appelbaum, E., and Shevchuk, I. (2009). Work process and quality of care in early childhood education: The role of job crafting. *The Academy of Management Journal*, p. 345.

Lesser, E. and Prusak, L. (1999). Communities of practice, social capital and organizational knowledge. *Information Systems Review*, 1(1), pp. 3–10.

Newman, M. (2020). *Networks*. Oxford: Oxford University Press.

Oshray, B. (2018). *Context, context, context*. Axminster: Triarchy Press.

Sherif, M. (1988). *The robbers cave experiment: Intergroup conflict and cooperation*. Middletown, CT: Wesleyan University Press.

Uphoff, N. and Wijayaratna, C.M. (2000). Demonstrated benefits from social capital: The productivity of farmer organizations in Gal Oya, Sri Lanka. *World Development* 28(11), pp. 1875–1890.

Chapter 9

Aghion, P. and Tirole, J. (1997). Formal and real authority in organizations. *Journal of Political Economy*.

Cross, R., Thomas, R., and Light, D. (2009). How "who you know" affects what you decide. *MIT Sloan Management Review*, 9 January.

Desjardins, J. (2021). *24 cognitive biases that are warping your perception of reality*. Available from: https://www.weforum.org/agenda/2021/11/humans-cognitive-bias-mistake [accessed 13 September 2022].

Edmondson, A. and Harvey, J-F. (2017). *Extreme teaming: Lessons in complex, cross-sector leadership*. Axminster: Emerald Publishing.

Heath, C. and Heath, D. (2013). *Decisive: How to make better choices in life and in work*. New York: Random House.

Kahneman, D. and Tversky, A. (1979). Prospect theory: An analysis of decision under risk, econometrica. *Econometric Society*, 47(2), 263–291.

Laloux, F. (2014). *Reinventing organizations*. Millis MA: Nelson Parker.

Lovallo, D. and Sibony, O. (2006). The case for behavioral strategy. *McKinsey Quarterly*.

Mintzberg, H. (1979). *The Structuring of organizations.* Hoboken NJ: Prentice Hall.

Morieux, Y. and Tollman, P. (2014). *Six simple rules: How to manage complexity without getting complicated.* Boston: Harvard Business Review Press.

Musser, C. and Sundaram, D. (2020). Steps to effective decision-making in organizations. *Workplace*, 13 May.

Powell, W.W. (1990). Neither market nor hierarchy: Network forms of organization. *Research in Organizational Behaviour*, 12, 295–336.

Rabois, K. (2016) *Should you delegate or do it yourself? A framework to help you decide.* Available from: https://medium.com/@DanlWebster/should-you-delegate-or-do-it-yourself-a-framework-to-help-you-decide-c806acbb32bb [accessed 14 September 2022].

Saks, A.M. (2017). Translating employee engagement research into practice. *Organizational Dynamics*, 46, pp. 76–86.

Thomas, K.W. and Velthouse, B.A. (1990). Cognitive elements of empowerment: An "interpretive" model of intrinsic task motivation. *Academy of Management Review*, 15(4), pp. 666–681.

Chapter 10

Archer, S. (2018). *Big potential.* Ebury Publishing.

Burt, R. (2001). The social capital of structural holes. In M.F. Guillen, R. Collins, P. England, and M. Meyer (Eds.), *New directions in economic sociology* (pp. 201–247). New York: Russell Sage Foundation.

Cross, R. (2004). *The hidden power of social networks.* Boston: Harvard Business Review Press.

Duhigg, C. (2016). What Google learned from its quest to build the perfect team. *New York Times Magazine*, 25 February.

Dunbar, R. (2022). *Friends: Understanding the power of our most important relationships.* London: Little, Brown Book Group Limited.

Edmondson, A. and Harvey, J-F. (2017). *Extreme teaming. Lessons in complex, cross-sector leadership.* Axminster: Emerald Publishing.

Haidt, J. (2012). *The righteous mind: Why good people are divided by politics and religion*. New York: Vintage Books.

Hefferman, M. (2015). It's time to forget the pecking order at work. *Ted Talk*. Available from: https://www.youtube.com/watch?v=Vyn_xLrtZaY [accessed 13 September 2022].

Jackson, M. (2019). *The human network: How your social position determines your power, beliefs, and behaviors*. New York: Vintage Books.

Kerr, S. (1995). On the folly of rewarding A while hoping for B. *The Academy of Management Executive, 9.*

Riedl, C., Kim, Y.J., Gupta, P., Malone, T.W., and Woolley, A.W. (2021). Quantifying collective intelligence in human groups. *Proceedings of the National Academy of Sciences,* May.

Surowiecki, J. (2005). *The wisdom of crowds*. New York: Anchor Books.

Chapter 11

Bodan, M., Dickau, D., and Mullady, I. (2020). Using adaptable organization network analysis to reveal patterns that drive inclusion. *HR Times*, 21 April.

Box, G. (1979). Robustness in the strategy of scientific model building. *Robustness in Statistics.*

Dutta, S. and Gardner, E. (2022). *The future of transformation is human*. Oxford: University of Oxford Press.

Dutton, J. (2020). *Dies Natalis 2020*. Erasmus University Rotterdam, November 6.

Harter, J.K. et al. (2020). Increased business value for positive job attitudes during economic recessions: A meta-analysis and SEM analysis. *Human Performance*, 33(4), pp. 307–330.

Kates, A. and Kesler, G. (2020). *Networked, scaled, and agile*. London: Kogan Page.

Lafley, A.G. and Martin, R. (2013). *Playing to win: How strategy really works*. Boston: Harvard Business Review Press.

Podolny, J.M. and Hansen, M.T. (2020). How Apple is organized for innovation. It's about experts leading experts. *HBR Magazine* November–December.

Prahalad, C.K. and Hamel, G. (1990). The core competence of the corporation archived 2014-07-14 at the wayback machine. *Harvard Business Review* 68(3), pp. 79–91.

Schneider, B. (2021). People management in work organizations: Fifty years of learnings. *Organizational Dynamics,* 50, pp. 1–10.

White, A. (2022). *The Future of transformation is human.* Available from: https://www.sbs.ox.ac.uk/oxford-answers/future-transformation-human [accessed 14 September 2022].

Chapter 12

Scholtes, P., Joiner, B.L., and Streibel, B.J. (2003). *The team handbook,* 3rd ed. Methuen, MA: GOAL/QPC.

Chapter 13

Burnett, B. and Evans, D. (2014). *Designing your life: How to build a well-lived, joyful life.* New York: Knopf.

Norman, D. (2013). *The design of everyday things.* New York: Basic Books.

Szczepanska, J. (2017). *Design thinking origin story plus some of the people who made it all happen* [online]. Available from: https://szczpanks.medium.com/design-thinking-where-it-came-from-and-the-type-of-people-who-made-it-all-happen-dc3a05411e53 [accessed 3 October 2022].

Chapter 14

Burt, R. (2001). The social capital of structural holes. In M.F. Guillen, R. Collins, P. England, and M. Meyer (Eds.), *New directions in economic sociology* (pp. 201–247). New York: Russell Sage Foundation.

Cross, R. (2021). *Beyond collaboration overload.* Boston: Harvard Business Review Press.

Dunbar, R. (2022). *Friends: Understanding the power of our most important relationships.* London: Little, Brown Book Group Limited.

Fealy, L. and Feinsod, R. (2022). How workforce rebalancing is building pressure in the talent pipeline. *EYGM Limited,* 18 April.

Haidt, J. (2012). *The righteous mind: Why good people are divided by politics and religion.* New York: Vintage Books.

Humanyze. (2022). *2021 future of work report.* Available from: https://humanyze.com/category/case-study/#list.[accessed 11 September 2022].

Jackson, M. (2019). *The human network: How your social position determines your power, beliefs, and behaviors.* New York: Vintage Books.

Morgan, J. (2012). *The collaborative organization: A strategic guide to solving your internal business challenges using emerging social and collaborative tools.* New York: McGraw Hill.

Schwartz, J. (2021). *Work disrupted: Opportunity, resilience, and growth in the accelerated future of work.* Hoboken: John Wiley & Sons.

New York Times. (2022). The magic of your first work friends. Available from: https://www.nytimes.com/2022/07/14/business/work-friends.html [accessed 9/14 September 2022].

Tomprou, M., Kim, Y. J., Chikersal, P., Woolley, A.W., and Dabbish, L.A. (2021). Speaking out of turn: How video conferencing reduces vocal synchrony and collective intelligence. *PLOS ONE* 16(3).

Wooley, A.W., Chabris, C.F., Pentland, A., Hashmi, N., and Malone, T.W. (2010). Evidence for a collective intelligence factor in the performance of human groups. *Science,* 330, pp. 686–688.

World Health Organization. (2019). *Burn-out an "occupational phenomenon": International classification of diseases.* Available from: https://www.who.int/news/item/28-05-2019-burn-out-an-occupational-phenomenon-international-classification-of-diseases [accessed 14 September 2022].

Wu, L., Waber B.N., Aral, S., Brynjolfsson, E., and Pentland, A. (2008). Mining face-to-face interaction networks using sociometric badges: Predicting productivity in an IT configuration task. Available from: https://ssrn.com/abstract=1130251 or http://dx.doi.org/10.2139/ssrn.1130251 [accessed 14 September 2022].

Yang, L., Holtz, D., Jaffe, S., Suri, S., Sinha, S., Weston, J., Joyce, C., Shah, N., Sherman, K., Hecht, B. and Teevan, J. (2021). The effects of remote work on collaboration among information workers. *Nature Human Behaviour,* [online] 6(6). doi:10.1038/s41562-021-01196-4.

Bibliography

Adams, J.S. (2020). *Equity theory: Process of model of motivation.* Available from: https://www.youtube.com/watch?v=ksnCw9-6vg7M [accessed 9/11/2022].

Adler, P.S. and Kwon, S-W. (2002). Social capital: Prospects for a new concept. *The Academy of Management Review* 27(1), pp. 17–40.

Aghion, P. and Tirole, J. (1997). Formal and real authority in organizations. *Journal of Political Economy.*

Archer, S. (2018). *Big potential.* Ebury Publishing.

Arena, M. (2018). *Adaptive space: How GM and other companies are positively disrupting themselves and transforming into agile organizations.* New York: McGraw-Hill Education.

Ariely, D. (2013). *What makes us feel good about our work?* Available from: https://www.ted.com/talks/dan_ariely_what_makes_us_feel_good_about_our_work?language=en#t-604603 [accessed 9/13/2022].

Baumeister, R. and Leary, M. (1995). The need to belong: Desire for interpersonal attachments as a fundamental human motivation. *Psychological Bulletin,* p. 497.

Berg, J.M., Dutton, J.E., and Wrzesniewski, A. (2001). Job crafting and meaningful work. *American Psychological Association.*

BetterUp. (2021). The value of belonging at work: New frontiers for inclusion in 2021 and beyond. Available from: https://grow.betterup .com/resources/the-value-of-belonging-at-work-the-business-case-for-investing-in-workplace-inclusion [accessed 12 September 2022].

Bhagat, S., Burke, M., and Diuk, C. (2016). *Three and a half degrees of separation*. Available from: https://research.facebook .com/blog/2016/02/three-and-a-half-degrees-of-separation [accessed 11 September 2022].

Bodan, M., Dickau, D., and Mullady, I. (2020). Using adaptable organization network analysis to reveal patterns that drive inclusion. *HR Times*, 21 April.

Box, G. (1979). Robustness in the strategy of scientific model building. *Robustness in Statistics*.

Brass, D.J. (1984). Being in the right place: a structural analysis of individual influence in an organization. *Administrative Science Quarterly*, 29, pp. 518–539.

Bregman, R. (2020). *Humankind: A hopeful history*. New York: Little, Brown and Company.

Buckingham, M. and Goodall, A. (2019). *Nine lies about work: A freethinking leader's guide to the real world*. Boston: Harvard Business Review Press.

Burnett, B. and Evans, D. (2014). *Designing your life: How to build a well-lived, joyful life*. New York: Knopf.

Burt, R. (2001). The social capital of structural holes. In M.F. Guillen, R. Collins, P. England, and M. Meyer (Eds.), *New directions in economic sociology* (pp. 201–247). New York: Russell Sage Foundation.

Burt, R. (2004). The social origins of good ideas. *American Journal of Sociology*.

Burt, R.S. (1992). *Structural holes: The social structure of competition*. Cambridge, MA: Harvard University Press.

Cable, D. (2019). *Alive at work: The neuroscience of helping your people love what they do*. Boston: Harvard Business Review Press.

Chow, W. S. and Chan, L. S. (2008). Social network, social trust and shared goals in organizational knowledge sharing. *Information & Management*, 45(7), pp. 458–465.

Claridge, T. (2004). *Social capital and natural resource management*. Unpublished Thesis.

Clarridge, T. (2020). Shared goals, shared purpose, shared vision. *Social Capital Research.*

Cole, N.L. (2020). *Units of analysis as related to sociology.* Available from: https://www.thoughtco.com/wh-units-of-analysis-matter-4019028 [accessed 11 September 2022].

Cross, R. (2004). *The hidden power of social networks.* Boston: Harvard Business Review Press.

Cross, R. (2021). *Beyond collaboration overload.* Boston: Harvard Business Review Press.

Cross, R., Thomas, R., and Light, D. (2009). How "who you know" affects what you decide. *MIT Sloan Management Review,* 9 January.

Culen, J. (2017). *Hierarchy, informal networks and how to navigate the full mess.* Available from: https://juliaculen.medium.com/hierarchy-informal-networks-and-how-to-navigate-the-full-mess-89d442b096a2 [accessed 11 September 2022].

Darwin, C. (1871). *The descent of man and selection in relation to sex.* Amherst NY: Prometheus Books.

De Smet, A., Kleinman, S., and Weerda, K. (2019). *The helix organization.* Available from: https://www.mckinsey.com/business-functions/people-and-organizational-performance/our-insights/the-helix-organization [accessed 11 September 2022].

Deming, W.E. (1993). *The new economics for industry, government, education.* Cambridge: Massachusetts Institute of Technology Center for Advanced Engineering Study.

Deming, W.E. (2018). *Out of the crisis.* Cambridge: The MIT Press.

Desjardins, J. (2021). *24 cognitive biases that are warping your perception of reality.* Available from: https://www.weforum.org/agenda/2021/11/humans-cognitive-bias-mistake [accessed 13 September 2022].

Dignan, A. (2019). *Brave new work: Are you ready to reinvent your organization?* New York: Portfolio/Penguin.

Duhigg, C. (2016). What Google learned from its quest to build the perfect team. *The New York Times Magazine,* 25 February. Available from: https://www.nytimes.com/2016/02/28/magazine/what-google-learned-from-its-quest-to-build-the-perfect-team.html [accessed: 29 August, 2022].

Duhigg, C. (2016). What Google learned from its quest to build the perfect team. *New York Times Magazine*, 25 February.

Dunbar, R. (2022). *Friends: Understanding the power of our most important relationships*. London: Little, Brown Book Group Limited.

Dutton, J. (2020). *Dies Natalis 2020*. Erasmus University Rotterdam, November 6.

Edmondson, A. and Harvey, J-F. (2017). *Extreme teaming. Lessons in complex, cross-sector leadership*. Bingley: Emerald Publishing.

FAQs for Organizations. (2016). *Vertical leverage*. Available from: http://www.faqsfororgs.com/vertical-leverage/ [accessed 11 September 2022].

Fass, C., Ginelli, M., and Turtle, B. (1996). *Six degrees of Kevin Bacon*. New York: Plume.

Fealy, L. and Feinsod, R. (2022). How workforce rebalancing is building pressure in the talent pipeline. *EYGM Limited*, 18 April.

Galbraith, J. (2014). *Designing organizations: Strategy, structure, and process at the business unit and enterprise levels*. San Francisco: Josey-Bass.

Gladwell, M. (2002). *The tipping point*. New York: Back Bay Books.

Goran, J., LaBerge, L., and Srinivasan, R. (2017) *Culture for a digital age*. Available from: https://www.mckinsey.com/business-functions/mckinsey-digital/our-insights/culture-for-a-digital-age [accessed 11 September 2022].

Greater Good. (2019). *Greater good: The science of a meaningful life* [online]. Available from: https://greatergood.berkeley.edu/ [accessed 9/11/2022].

Haidt, J. (2012). *The righteous mind: Why good people are divided by politics and religion*. New York: Vintage Books.

Hamel, G. and Zanini, M. (2020). *Humanocracy*. Boston: Harvard Business Review Press.

Hannan, M.T. and Freeman, J. (1984). Structural inertia and organizational change. *American Sociological Review*.

Hare, B. and Woods, V. (2020). *Survival of the friendliest: Understanding our origins and rediscovering our common humanity*. New York: Random House.

Harris, M. and Tayler, B. (2019). Don't let metrics undermine your business. *Harvard Business Review*, September–October.

Harter, J.K. et al. (2020). Increased business value for positive job attitudes during economic recessions: A meta-analysis and SEM analysis. *Human Performance*, 33(4), pp. 307–330.

Heath, C. and Heath, D. (2013). *Decisive: How to make better choices in life and in work*. New York: Random House.

Hefferman, M. (2015). It's time to forget the pecking order at work. *Ted Talk*. Available from: https://www.youtube.com/watch?v=Vyn_xLrtZaY [accessed 13 September 2022].

Hörrmann, G. and Tiby, C. (1990). Project Management made correctly. *Management of the high-performance organization*. Wiesbaden: pp. 73–91. (In German).

Humanyze. (2022). *2021 future of work report*. Available from: https://humanyze.com/category/case-study/#list. [accessed 11 September 2022].

Islam, G. (2014). Social identity theory. *Encyclopedia of Critical Psychology*. New York: Springer.

Jackson, M. (2019). *The human network: How your social position determines your power, beliefs, and behaviors*. New York: Vintage Books.

Jaques, E. (1990). In praise of hierarchy. *Harvard Business Review*, 68(1), pp. 127–133.

Kates, A. and Kesler, G. (2020). *Networked, scaled, and agile*. London: Kogan Page.

Kates, A., Kesler, G., and DiMartino, M, (2021). *Networked, scaled, and agile*. London: Kogan Page Ltd.

Kerr, S. (1995). On the folly of rewarding A while hoping for B. *The Academy of Management Executive*, 9.

King, H. (2020). Flow: The emerging paradigm. *Henry King*, 31 July.

Kleiner, A. (2002). *Karen Stephenson's quantum theory of trust*. Available from: https://www.strategy-business.com/article/20964 [accessed 29 August 2022].

Kohn, A. (2018). *Punished by rewards: Twenty-fifth anniversary edition: The trouble with gold stars, incentive plans, A's, praise, and other bribes.* Boston: Mariner Books.

Krackhardt, D. and Hansen, J. (1993). *Informal networks: The company behind the chart*. Available from: https://hbr.org/1993/07/informal-networks-the-company-behind-the-chart [accessed 13 September 2022].

Krebs, V. (2007). Managing 21st century organizations. *IHRIM Journal*, XI(4).

Lafley, A.G. and Martin, R. (2013). *Playing to win: How strategy really works*. Boston: Harvard Business Review Press.

Laloux, F. (2014). *Reinventing organizations*. Millis MA: Nelson Parker.

Leana, C., Appelbaum, E., and Shevchuk, I. (2009). Work process and quality of care in early childhood education: The role of job crafting. *The Academy of Management Journal*, p. 345.

Lencioni, P. (2006). *Silos, politics, and turf wars*. San Francisco: Jossey-Bass.

Lesser, E. and Prusak, L. (1999). Communities of practice, social capital and organizational knowledge. *Information Systems Review*, 1(1), pp. 3–10.

Levitin, D.J. (2015). *The organized mind: Thinking straight in the age of information overload*. New York: Dutton.

Lin, N. (2001). *Social capital: A theory of social structure and action*. Cambridge: Cambridge University Press.

Lovallo, D. and Sibony, O. (2006). The case for behavioral strategy. *McKinsey Quarterly*.

McChrystal, S. (2015). *Team of teams*. New York: Portfolio/Penguin.

McDowell, T. (2016). *Organizational network analysis*. Available from: https://www2.deloitte.com/content/dam/Deloitte/us/Documents/human-capital/us-cons-organizational-network-analysis.pdf [accessed 11 September 2022].

Meadows, D. (2008). *Thinking in systems: A primer.* White River Junstion,VT: Sustainability Institute, p. 14.

Milgram, S. (1967). The small world problem. *Psychology Today,* 2, pp. 60–67.

Minnaar, J. and de Morree, P. (2019). *Corporate rebels: Make work more fun.* New York: Corporate Rebels Nederland BV.

Mintzberg, H. (1979). *The Structuring of organizations.* Hoboken NJ: Prentice Hall.

Mochari, I. (2014). *The case for hierarchy.* Available from: https://www .inc.com/ilan-mochari/case-for-hierarchy.html [accessed 11 September 2022].

Morgan, J. (2012). *The collaborative organization:A strategic guide to solving your internal business challenges using emerging social and collaborative tools.* New York: McGraw Hill.

Morieux, Y. (2014). *As work gets more complex, 6 rules to simplify.* Available from: https://www.youtube.com/watch?v=0MD4- Ymjyc2I [accessed 11 September 2022].

Morieux, Y. and Tollman, P. (2014). *Six simple rules: How to manage complexity without getting complicated.* Boston: Harvard Business Review Press.

Musser, C. and Sundaram, D. (2020). Steps to effective decision-making in organizations. *Workplace,* 13 May.

National Institutes of Health. (2008). *Human brain appears "hard-wired" for hierarchy.* Available from: https://www.nih.gov/news-events/news-releases/human-brain-appears-hard-wired-hierarchy [accessed 10 September 2022].

New York Times. (2022). The magic of your first work friends. Available from: https://www.nytimes.com/2022/07/14/business/work-friends.html [accessed 9/14 September 2022].

Newman, M. (2020). *Networks.* Oxford: Oxford University Press.

Nicholson, N. (1998). How hardwired is human behavior? *HBR Magazine,* July–August.

Norman, D. (2013). *The design of everyday things.* New York: Basic Books.

O'Boyle, E. and Aguinis, A. (2012). The best and the rest: Revisiting the norm of normality of individual performance. *Personnel Psychology*.

Oshray, B. (2018). *Context, context, context: How our blindness to context cripples even the smartest organizations*. Axminster: Triarchy Press.

Pflaeging, N. (2020). *Organize for complexity*. BetaCodex Publishing, p. 19.

Pink, D. (2011). *Drive: The surprising truth about what motivates us*. New York: Riverhead Books.

Podolny, J.M. and Hansen, M.T. (2020). How Apple is organized for innovation: It's about experts leading experts. *HBR Magazine*, November–December.

Powell, W. (1990). Neither market nor hierarchy: Network forms of organization 12. *Research in Organizational Behaviour*, pp. 295–336.

Prahalad, C.K. and Hamel, G. (1990). The core competence of the corporation archived 2014-07-14 at the wayback machine. *Harvard Business Review* 68(3), pp. 79–91.

Rabois, K. (2016). *Should you delegate or do it yourself? A framework to help you decide*. Available from: https://medium.com/@DanlWebster/should-you-delegate-or-do-it-yourself-a-framework-to-help-you-decide-c806acbb32bb [accessed 14 September 2022].

Riedl, C., Kim, Y.J., Gupta, P., Malone, T.W., and Woolley, A.W. (2021). Quantifying collective intelligence in human groups. *Proceedings of the National Academy of Sciences,* May.

Robbins, T. (2007). *Awaken the giant within*. New York: Simon & Schuster.

Romero, D.M., Uzzi, B., and Kleinberg, J. (2016). Social networks under stress. *Social and Information Networks*.

Saks, A.M. (2017). Translating employee engagement research into practice. *Organizational Dynamics*, 46, pp. 76–86.

Schneider, B. (2021). People management in work organizations: Fifty years of learnings. *Organizational Dynamics,* 50, pp. 1–10.

Scholtes, P., Joiner, B.L., and Streibel, B.J. (2003). *The team handbook,* 3rd ed. Methuen, MA: GOAL/QPC.

Schwartz, J. (2021). *Work disrupted: Opportunity, resilience, and growth in the accelerated future of work.* Hoboken: John Wiley & Sons.

Schwartz, J. et al. (2020). The compensation conundrum. *Deloitte,* 15 May.

Shapiro, C. and Varian, H. (1990). *Information rules: A strategic guide to the network economy.* Boston: Harvard Business School Press.

Sherif, M. (1988). *The robbers cave experiment: Intergroup conflict and cooperation.* Middletown, CT: Wesleyan University Press.

Shirky, C. (2008). *Here comes everybody: The power of organizing without organizations.* New York: Penguin Books.

Soda, G. and Zaheer, A. (2012). A network perspective on organizational architecture: performance effects of the interplay of formal and informal organization. *Strategic Management Journal.*

Stephenson, K. (2005). Trafficking in trust: The DNA of social capital. In L. Coughlin, E. Wingard, and K. Hollihan (Eds.), *Enlightened power: How women are transforming the practice of leadership* (pp. 243–266). San Francisco: Jossey-Bass.

Stephenson, K. (2021). Social capital analysis: The newest and strongest tool for driving strategic impact. *NetForm Resources,* November 24.

Surowiecki, J. (2005). *The wisdom of crowds.* New York: Anchor Books.

Szczepanska, J. (2017). *Design thinking origin story plus some of the people who made it all happen* [online]. Available from: https://szczpanks. medium.com/design-thinking-where-it-came-from-and-the-type-of-people-who-made-it-all-happen-dc3a05411e53 [accessed 3 October 2022].

Thomas, K.W. and Velthouse, B.A. (1990). Cognitive elements of empowerment: An "interpretive" model of intrinsic task motivation. *Academy of Management Review,* 15(4), pp. 666–681.

Tomprou, M., Kim, Y. J., Chikersal, P., Woolley, A.W., and Dabbish, L.A. (2021). Speaking out of turn: How video conferencing reduces vocal synchrony and collective intelligence. *PLOS ONE* 16(3).

Townsend, R.C. and Bennis, W. (2007). *Up the organization: How to stop the corporation from stifling people and strangling profits.* New York: John Wiley & Sons.

Turchin, P. (2020, December). The next decade could be even worse. *The Atlantic.*

Uphoff, N. and Wijayaratna, C.M. (2000). Demonstrated benefits from social capital: The productivity of farmer organizations in Gal Oya, Sri Lanka. *World Development* 28(11), pp. 1875–1890.

Uzzi, B. (1997). Social structure and competition in interfirm networks: the paradox of embeddedness. *Administrative Science Quarterly.* 42, pp. 35–67.

Weber, M. (2022). *Chain of command principle.* Available from: https://www.referenceforbusiness.com/management/Bun-Comp/Chain-of-Command-Principle.html [accessed 11 September 2022].

Weller, C. (2019). *3 big ideas to revolutionize performance conversations.* Available from: https://neuroleadership.com/your-brain-at-work/performance-conversations-3-big-ideas [accessed 11 September 2022].

White, A. (2022). *The Future of transformation is human.* Available from: https://www.sbs.ox.ac.uk/oxford-answers/future-transformation-human [accessed 14 September 2022].

Wigert, B. (2020). *Employee burnout: The biggest myth.* Available from: https://www.gallup.com/workplace/288539/employee-burnout-biggest-myth.aspx. [accessed 11 September 2022].

Wooley, A.W., Chabris, C.F., Pentland, A., Hashmi, N., and Malone, T.W. (2010). Evidence for a collective intelligence factor in the performance of human groups. *Science,* 330, pp. 686–688.

World Health Organization. (2019). *Burn-out an "occupational phenomenon": International classification of diseases.* Available from: https://www.who.int/news/item/28-05-2019-burn-out-an-occupational-phenomenon-international-classification-of-diseases [accessed 14 September 2022].

Wu, L., Waber B.N., Aral, S., Brynjolfsson, E., and Pentland, A. (2008). Mining face-to-face interaction networks using sociometric badges: Predicting productivity in an IT configuration task. Available from: https://ssrn.com/abstract=1130251 or http://dx.doi.org/10.2139/ssrn.1130251 [accessed 14 September 2022].

About the Author

Tiffany McDowell, PhD, is a principal at Ernst and Young, LLP. She has advised dozens of Fortune 500 CXOs on the topic of organization design, published in academic journals and in *Harvard Business Review* on innovations in the field of organizational design, and taught the subject at multiple universities over the years. Tiffany is uniquely positioned to be the authority on this topic, having built one of the largest and most successful organization design practices in the world by bringing scientifically proven ideas together with a long and successful consulting career. She completed her BA in psychology at the University of British Columbia, her MBA at Simon Fraser University, and her PhD in industrial psychology at the California School of Professional Psychology. Note the views in the book are the author's views and do not necessarily reflect the views of other parties.

Acknowledgments

I started working when I was 14 as a tour guide (my first job in a nice suit and high heels, the start of a lifelong obsession with both). Not only did I quickly realize that I was going to have to spend a LOT of time at work, for MOST of my life, but I decided that I only wanted to work if the work I was doing was fun.

And some of the work I did—be it as a roller-skating waitress or a vendor of handmade hats at Grateful Dead shows—was very fun indeed. Some of it, however, such as doing data entry at a bank, was not fun at all. But it was my experience of the contrast between the two that eventually—and I do mean eventually, just ask my dad—led me to write my doctoral dissertation, "How to Have Fun at Work."

My hypothesis was that there are fun companies and there are fun people (like me!). However, I was only able to prove the first part. My data strongly showed support for a fun organizational climate and the benefits this positive environment has on business performance. But it turns out, to my surprise, being a "fun person" does not impact a person's experience of how enjoyable their work is. As such, I have spent my career working with organizations to create an environment for their employees that is genuinely fun. With this book, I hope more organizations will find a way to make the work their employees do be genuinely enjoyable, too.

I was able to write this book due to the love and support of my family, friends, and colleagues. First and foremost, it would not have been possible without the support of my wonderful husband Jay, who took on extra parenting our three beautiful children and even extracurricular writing duties to help me get it to the finish line, and did so with love, every step of the way. Thank you honey.

I have dedicated this book to my father Mickey McDowell, who I am immensely grateful for. I am also grateful for my sister Kylie and my brother Brogan, for all of my Vancouver- and California-based girlfriends (I don't have room to name you all, but you know who you are!), and for my brilliant colleagues both past and present. I am extremely thankful for the legacies of my sister Brittany and my best friend Darcy, and for the example set by my extraordinary mother, Gerry. Finally, I appreciate the support of Ernst & Young LLP (EY US), where I am proud to be a principal.

I am especially indebted to one person in particular, India Mullady. She has been my partner in crime for over a decade, selflessly supporting me in life and in work, and sacrificing countless hours of sleep to travel cross-country with me in a quest to perfect the ideas laid out in this book and use them to support our clients. She has been my thought partner, idea challenger, and most importantly, my dear friend. India, thank you. You truly make work fun, and I look forward to another decade of us working while having fun together!

Index

A

Accountability, 100t, 109–110
  ability, 99
  absence, 10
  basis, 99
  central accountability, 102–103
  culture, 136
  definition, 98–100
  environment, fostering, 33
  flow, 100
  identification, 33
  perception, creation, 71
Accountable blueprint, 172–173
Action, coordination (efficiency), 93
Adams, John Stacey, 14
Adaptive challenges, 167
Adaptive Space (Arena), 51
Adverse events, 37
Affective processes, shift, 52
Aghion, Philippe, 101
Agile methodology, 76
Agile teams, introduction, 102
Algorithms, usage, 39
Alive at Work (Cable), 74, 78
All-hands webcasts, usage, 162
Altruists, creation, 18
American Customer Satisfaction Index, 135
Anchoring bias, example, 104f

Archer, Shawn, 116
Architecting, 100
  personnel, selection, 153–154
Architecture, purpose/utility (interrelation-
    ship), 122f, 133
Arena, Michael, 51
Ariely, Dan, 69
Attention, 68–70
Authority, 98–100, 100t
  domain authority, 39–40
  focus, 98
  identification, 33
  ladders, responsibility (interplay), 102
Authority/empowerment (A/E)
  exercise, 109f
Authority/empowerment (A/E)
  method, 172
Autonomy
  absence, 10
  support, 144–145
  unleashing, 101

B

Back office, front office (contrast), 130–131
Backstabbing, absence, 118
Balanced network, unbalanced network
    (contrast), 46f
Baumeister, Roy, 94

209

Behavioral biases, 45, 104–105
Belonging
  feelings (production), integration
    (impact), 84
  importance, question, 94–95
  social belonging, dependence, 16
Berg, Justin M., 96
BetterUp, workplace study, 94
Biases, 104
Big potential, 116–117
Big Potential (Archer), 116
Bonding gap (bridging), events (usage), 166
Bonuses, size (increase), 50
Bottom-up approach, 147
Bottom-up decision-making, 172–173
Boundaries, defining (clarity), 112–113
Boundary spanning, 71, 114
Brand
  change, 2
  management/recognition, 34
Bregman, Rutger, 88, 90
Bridging capital, 43, 49, 161
Bridging connections, increase, 159
Buckingham, Marcus, 74, 75
Burnout, 163
Burt, Ronald, 49, 51, 114, 159
Business
  belonging, importance (question), 94–95
  history, 129–130
  model, 124, 141–142
  outcomes, components, 21
  running, smoothness, 31
Business units (BUs), characteristic, 80–81

C
Cable, Can, 74, 78
Capability, 125–127
Capital
  human capital, return on investment, 50
  sharing, 34
  social capital benefits, 49–52
Celebrations, usage, 13
Central accountability, 102–103

Central/decentral trade-offs, 103t
Chain of command, uncertainty, 30
Changes, planning/blueprinting, 13
Coffee break, usage, 146
Cognitive processes, shift, 52
Collaboration, 80, 164–165
  encouragement, 26
  preference, 112
  problems, 10, 13, 21
  structuring, 153
Collaborative approaches, 73
Collaborative crafting, 95–96
Collaborative culture, 4
Collaborative mindset, 33
Collaborative profit and loss (collaborative
    P&L), 72–74
Collaborative skill building, 72
Collective incentives, 79–81
Collective intelligence (CI), 117, 161–165
Collective mental model, development, 114
Commitments
  agreement, defining, 177–178
  web, example, 102f
Communication, 142–143
  cost savings, 46
  disruption, 45
  limiting, 13
  progress source, 114
Communities of practice (intervention
    technique), 64
Community boundaries, importance, 47–48
Company growth, 2
Company-wide improvements, 1
Company-wide performance numbers,
    basis, 73–74
Compensation, performance
    (decoupling), 79
Complexity, reduction, 62
Confirmation bias, 105
Conflict, breeding, 49
Connection, cost, 27–28
Consistency, 61–62
Context, Context, Context (Oshray), 84

Context, impact, 146
Cooperating, rewards, 17–18
"Core Competence of the Corporation,
    The" (Prahalad/Hamel), 126
Core competencies, criteria fulfillment, 126
Core networks, increase, 57
Corporate cultures, differences, 84
Correlation neglect, 45
COVID-19 pandemic, impact, 157, 162
Creative solutions, generation, 50
Cross-boundary efforts, requirement
    (absence), 119
Cross-boundary teams, innovation
    leverage, 114
Crosscut, addition, 56f
Cross-functional networks, reciprocal
    workflows (impact), 62
Cross-functional teams, participation, 84
Cross-group agreements, disruption, 73
Cross, Rob, 16
Cross-selling strategy, 66
Culture, 134–136
    decisions, alignment, 107
Customer demands, meeting, 2

D
Darwin, Charles, 90–91, 115
Day-to-day activities, completion, 32
Deals, closing (acceleration), 50
Decentral empowerment, 102–103
Decision-making
    collaboration, 106
    model, autonomy (support), 144–145
    procedures, establishment/adherence, 107
Decisions
    alignment, 102–103
    bias, 103–105
    communication, 107
    foundation/development/realization, 107
    frameworks, 108–110
    rights, 105–107, 172
Decisive (Heath/Heath), 107
DeGroot learning, 45–46

Delegation, timing, 108t
Deming, W. Edwards, 9
Design
    decisions, behavior link (absence), 1–3
    principles, 143, 169–170
    solutions, focus, 1, 4–5
    support, 21, 23
    testable criteria, principles
        (alignment), 170
    thinking, deployment, 151–152
    trade-offs, 20
Designing Your Life (Burnett/Evans), 152
Design of Everyday Things, the (Norman),
    151
Diffusion, impact, 51
DiMartino, Michelle, 72, 126
Discover-build-scale framework,
    creation, 166
Disruption, impact, 51
Distributed networks, building, 63–64
Distrust, breeding, 49
Domain authority, 39–40
Dotted-line accountability, absence, 36
Dotted-line reporting, 26, 31, 128–129
Double counting, 45–47
Drive (Pink), 14, 77
Drucker, Peter, 67
Dunbar, Robin, 118
Dutton, Jane E., 96
Dysfunctional silos, connection, 63

E
Echo chambers, 6, 43, 45–48, 117
Ecosystem choices, 123
Edmondson, Amy, 119
Effort, divergence, 32
Egocentric network view, fooling, 40
Employees
    interaction, 34
    joint decision-making, 62
    morale, damage, 70
Employer brand, discussion, 3
Empowered blueprint, 172–173

Empowerment
absence, 10, 17–18
authority/empowerment (A/E)
exercise, 109f
decentral empowerment, 102–103
impact, 110
level, 21, 23
team empowerment, 110, 153
"Empowerment by leadership," operation-
alization, 110
Engagement, 77–78, 142–143
Enterprise mindset, 4, 27, 72
Enterprise strategy, focus, 141–142
Environment, change (rapidity), 31
Equity theory, 14
Excitement, feeling, 77–78
Executive leaders, placement, 125
Expectations, clarity (importance), 26
Expenses, sharing, 34
Experience, 134–136
External motivators, 31

F
Fate, shared sense, 86, 89–91
Feedback, 75
attention, equivalence, 68
in-the-moment feedback, 70
Fight-or-flight mode, 14
Flat lattice, 117
Flat structure, advantages/disadvantages, 29
Flat structures, tall structures, contrast, 29f
Follow-through, ensuring, 107
Formal hierarchy, 60t
Formal structure, usefulness, 33
Forums, organizing, 146
Foundation, importance, 15
Four Factor Theory of Leadership, 152
Friction, creation, 27
Front office, back office (contrast), 130–131
Functional barriers, impact, 32f
Functional boundaries, 98
Functional capabilities, combination, 131
Future circumstances, awareness, 34

G
Gatekeepers, 42, 45, 51
Pulsetakers, combination, 54
Gladwell, Malcolm, 45
Goals
mental models, equivalence, 93
shared goals, individual goals
(contrast), 74–76
unification, 86
Goodall, Ashley, 74, 75
Gore, Bill, 117
Gore-Tex, founding, 117
Governance, alternative approach, 172
Group-level dynamics, 10
Groups
affinity, amplification, 86–91
competition, 48
disunity, 89
life, advantages, 90
members, 21
role, 87
wisdom, timing, 113–114
Groupthink, 6

H
Haidt, Jonathan, 15, 18, 89, 165
Hamel, Gary, 7, 126
Harris Reputation Quotient, 135
Heath, Chip/Dan, 107
Heffernan, Margaret, 115
Hierarchical barriers, 32f
work network, impact, 6
Hierarchical organization, strength, 33
Hierarchy, 33–34
approach, change, 35–36
arrangement, 130f
building, 39, 153
business outcome component,
21, 25, 27–28
changes, 140
construction, methods, 125
decision-making authority, 101
decisions, alignment, 102–103

elegance, understanding, 11
impact, 28
moves, making, 131
networks, contrast, 59
power, equivalence (theory), 10
strength, 60
structures, networks (dynamic inter-action), 59
structuring, 127
value, 11
High-performance organizations, collaboration (emphasis), 80
Home-based teams, impact, 62
Homophily, 43, 47–49, 84, 159
increase, 52
self-reinforcement, 48
side effects, damage (counteracting), 53
tendency, 7–8
Horizontal networks (power), design (ignoring), 1, 5–7
Horizontal roles, success, 134
Horizontal structures, work safety (feeling), 34
Hub-and-spoke system, 41
Hubs, 41–42, 45, 47, 51
Human capital, return on investment, 50
Human evolution, groups (role), 87
Humanity, connections-45, 43
Humankind (Bregman), 88, 90
Human life, opportunities, 18
Human network strategies, example, 41f
Humanocracy (Hamel/Zanini), 7
Human Resources (HR) professional, role, 155–156
Human transformation, 136

I
Identity
conflict, 85
sense, 36
Implicit bias, coaching, 4
Import-export business, 49

Individual goals, shared goals (contrast), 74–76
Individual motivation, increase, 110
Individual performance, 61
shared goals, contrast, 146–148
targets, 72
Individual profit and loss (individual P&L), 112
Individual rewards, transformation, 78–79
Individuals
design solutions focus, 1, 4–5
peopletecture, usage, 139
Influencers, 42–43, 47
identification/engagement, 145
Influencing power (determination), networks (impact), 390
Informal interactions, 63
fostering, 146
Informal meetings, 63, 146
Informal networks, 60t
Information
access, 55
aggregation, network structuring, 46
Information Age, 123
In-group members, 85–86
Innovation, 38
encouragement, location, 127
leverage, 114
occurrence, 6
Innovative organization, creation, 54
Intangible connections, 38–39
Integrated Strategic Choice Cascade, 124, 133
Integration, location (determination), 126
Intelligence quotient (IQ), 5
Interaction, patterns, 92
Inter-functional teams, creation, 63, 146
Intergroup behavior, explanation, 85
Interpersonal communication skills, teaching, 4
Intervention techniques, 63–64
Intrinsic motivation, expression (enabling), 110

J

Jackson, Mathew, 48
Jaques, Elliott, 11, 28
Jobs, 143
  creation, 57, 153
  defining, 91
  design, role crafting (contrast), 170
  grade, association, 93
  people, assignment, 91
  roles, contrast, 91–92
  rotation, 63, 146
  structural characteristics, 95
Jobs, Steve, 73

K

Kahneman, Daniel, 103
Kates, Amy, 72, 126
Kerr, Steven, 67, 119
Kesler, Greg, 72, 126
Kleinberg, Jon, 52
Knowledge
  access, 55
  clusters, intersection, 6
  diversity, impact, 113
  exchange, 38–39
  pathways, 53
  sharing, 51
  success, 42
Kohn, Alfie, 77
Krebs, Valdis, 54

L

Laloux, Frédéric, 13
Leaders, change, 2
Leadership, 31, 134–136
  change, absence, 84
  development, investment, 5
  four factor theory, 152
Lean Six Sigma, 7
Learning
  inhibition, 68
  leverage, 94–95
Leary, Mark, 94
Legacy organizations, 84

Lencioni, Patrick, 32
Leverage, improvement, 146
Levitin, Daniel, 30
Likert, Rensis, 152
Limbic brain, reliance, 14
Lincoln, Abraham, 88
Line-of-sight approaches, 73
Long-term customer relationships,
  building, 66–67
Lovallo, Dan, 105
Loyalty, feelings, 91
Loyalty/betrayal model (Haidt), 15

M

Machiavelli, 42
Macro decisions, occurrence, 1–2
Macro-level choices, 121
Macro model choices, 125
Management Labs, 7
Managers
  joint decision-making, 62
  peopletecture, usage, 139
Market (hierarchy construction
  method), 125
Markets, access, 126
Martin, Roger, 124, 133
Matrix manager, meetings, 27
Matrix organizations, managers/supervisors
  (presence), 31
Matrix reporting, 26, 128
McCallum, Daniel, 11
McChrystal, Stanley, 28
Meadows, Donella, 19
Measurement
  business outcome component, 21, 65
  performance measurement, necessity
    (question), 66–68
  system measurement, 70–72
Membership
  business outcome component, 21, 83
  design, 21, 23
  fate, shared sense, 86, 89–91
  similarity/competition, 86–88
Meta-analysis, usage, 113

Metrics, value-destroying effects, 72
Microsoft Teams, usage, 53
Milgram, Stanley, 43
Mission, pursuit, 28
Mission-based teams, introduction, 102
Moggridge, Bill, 152
Morale
  damage, 70
  improvement, 28
  problem, breeding, 49
Morieux, Yves, 13
Motivated reasoning (bias), 104
Motivation, rewards (link), 77–78
Motorola, four-point rating scale
  (disbanding), 79
Multilevel selection, 90, 115
Multiple social identities, 85
Mutual kindness, increase, 88

N
Negativity bias, concept, 74
Networked, Scaled, and Agile (Kates/Kesler/
  DiMartino), 72, 126
Networks
  analysis, 5–6
  analytics, 63
  business outcome component, 21, 37
  change, process, 52–53, 62
  characteristics, 38–39
  collaboration, structuring, 153
  complexity, 60
  data, accessibility (ease), 53
  decisions, alignment, 102–103
  density, increase, 52
  dimensions, revelation, 39
  divisions, 48
  dynamics, understanding, 52
  efficiency, connection, 56–57
  hierarchy, contrast, 59
  hierarchy structure, dynamic
    interaction, 59
  human network strategies, example, 41f
  insights, usage, 119
  intervention, 46

  knowledge, 40, 53–57, 145–146
  patterns, 54
  proximity, people density, 86
  reaction, 52
  repair, 57–58
  roles, 40–43
  theory, usage, 137
  unbalanced network, balanced network
    (contrast), 46f
Networks (Newman), 95
NeuroLeadership Institute, 14
Newman, Mark, 95
Nine Lies About Work (Buckingham/
  Goodall), 74
Noise, filtration, 53
Non-value-adding activities, 7
Norman, Don, 151

O
Occupy Wall Street movement, 14
Office spaces, design/adjustment/
  creation, 146, 158
Onboarding, 40
Open-source arrangement, setup, 123
Operating model, meaning, 125
Operative islands, functional/hierarchical
  barriers (impact), 32f
Opinions, sharing (encouragement), 107
Organizational life, decisions (impor-
  tance), 124
Organizational purpose, decisions
  (alignment), 107
Organizational scar tissue, removal, 153
Organizational settings, status
  (obtaining), 11
Organizational theory, 129–130
Organization design, 50, 95–96,
  118–120, 128
  capability, building (process), 154–156
  new approach, 152–153
  problems, 7–8
  work, harmony, 8
Organization network analysis
  (ONA), 39–40

Organizations, 3
charts, 6, 28–29
command-and-control type, 134–135
efficiency, design, 48
focus, impact, 28
intervention, 8
organization chart (McCallum/Henshaw design), 12f
problems, determination, 127–130
purpose, 34, 121, 132
size, importance, 117–118
structures, differences, 28–31
team member interpretation, purpose (impact), 123
value, providing, 34
Organized Mind, The (Levitin), 30
Organizing
core question, 4–5
future, 157
initiation point, 149
Out-group members, 85–86
Output, maximization, 5
Ownership
absence, 10–13, 21
clarity, 153

P
Pay unfairness, perception, 10, 14
Peers, self-organization, 10
People
attention, importance, 69–70
characteristics, defining, 8
connections, methods, 43f
identity, change/evolution (transition period), 86
interaction, repetition, 86
jobs assignment, 91
management confidence, 35
performance, ignoring (problem), 70
small-world network, 44f
trust, tracking, 59
Peopletecture, 136, 139, 142, 148

Peopletecture Model, 19, 133, 143, 153
connections, 23f
implementation, 121
origins, 22t
Perceived customer benefits, contribution, 126
Perception, anchoring bias (example), 104f
Performance
compensation, decoupling, 79
differences, 37
evaluations, receiving, 50
hindrance, 145
management, 70, 75
meaning (attachment), shared goals (usage), 80
measurement, necessity (question), 66–68
negative influence, 78
objectives/incentives (intervention technique), 63
payment, problem, 78
review process, events, 69
reviews, 68–69
unfairness, perception, 10, 14
Permanent work groups, 63, 146
Pflaeging, Niels, 20
Pink, Daniel H., 14, 77, 78
Plan of action, development, 107
Playing to Win (Martin), 124
Polarization, increase, 52
Power, enhancement, 49
Prahalad, C.K., 126
Primary axis, 125–127
Primary value choices, determination, 126
Problems, solving, 9
Productivity
increase, 75
maximization, 5
Product sales, top-line revenue targets (sharing), 73
Profit and loss (P&L), 65
accountability, 71
responsibilities, 73
statement, usage, 147

system measurement, 70–72
Project Aristotle (Google), 116
Project managers, performance
    (improvement), 50
Project teams, network map, 55f
Promotions, acceleration, 50
Proximity, impact, 164
Psychology of Everyday Things, The
    (Norman), 151
Pulsetakers, 42, 51
    Gatekeepers, combination, 54
Purpose, 121–123, 133, 146, 153–154
    articulation, 133
    utility/architecture,
        interrelationship, 122f

R
Radical transparency, providing, 153
Rating pattern, 68–69
Reciprocal workflows, impact, 62
Redesign trade-offs, 20
Relational crafting, 95
Relationships
    co-creation, 143–144
    forging/formation/mainte-
        nance, 140, 159
    horizontal network, structuring, 129
    informal networks, 38
Reorganization
    company desire, 2
    limitation, 20
Research and development, increase, 50
Resentment, breeding, 49
Resources, sharing, 34
Responsibility, 21, 100t, 165
    business outcome component, 21, 97
    clarity, absence, 26
    cultivation, 109
    definition, 98–100
    division, 11–12
    focus, 98
Responsible, accountable, consulted, and
    informed (RACI), 107–108

Return-to-office policies, face-to-face
    interactions (benefits), 160–161
Rewards
    individual rewards, transformation, 78–79
    motivation, link, 77–78
    purpose, 79
Right problems, solving, 9
Roadblocks, removal, 34
Rock, David, 14
Role crafting, 21, 23, 141
    approach/definition, 171
    job design, contrast, 170
    template, 170–171
Roles, 93, 154–155
    assigning, 92
    co-creation, 143–144
    jobs, contrast, 91–92
    overlap, problems, 10, 13, 21
    social capital, contrast, 93–94
Romero, Daniel, 52

S
Sales, marketing (contrast), 48
Schneider, Ben, 135
Schwartz, Jeff, 163
Scrum teams, 76
Self-managing teams, introduction, 102
Self-organization, 10
Senior leadership, strategy
    (implementation), 51
Separation, location (determination),
    126
Shared destiny, sense, 89
Shared goals
    cascading, 147
    establishment, 146–148
    existence, 89
    individual goals, contrast, 74–76
    individual performance, contrast,
        146–148
    usage, 80
    value, 76
Shared mental model, 36

Sherif, Muzafer, 86–87
Sibony, Olivier, 105
Silos, 48–49
    connection, network knowledge, 145–146
    dysfunctional silos, connection, 63
    problems, 63
    trap, 32–33, 145
Six Degrees of Separation (Fass/Ginelli/
    Turtle), 43
Slack, usage, 53
Small-world network, 43–44, 44f, 55–56
Social belonging, dependence, 16
Social capital, 94, 158–160
    benefits, 49–52
    bridging, 146
    building/manifesting, 92
    dominant effect, 50
    roles, contrast, 93–94
Social categorization theory, 85
Social connections, 116–117
    absence, 10, 15–17, 21
    improvement, 153
Social environment, changes (impact), 17
Social identity theory, 85
Social isolation, impact, 163
Social media influencers, 47
Social networks, teaming, 21
Social Networks Under Stress (Romero/Uzzi/
    Kleinberg), 52
Social organization, cost (reduction), 94
Social Origins of Good Ideas, The (Burt), 49
Social relations, social capital creation, 50
Social sensitivity, 116–117
Social structures, analysis, 5
Social ties, interest, 15–16
Solidarity, 88, 146
Solution (hierarchy construction
    method), 125
Solutioning, improvement process, 176
Specialization, encouragement, 29
Stability, maximization, 5
Standards, global set, 111
Stephenson, Karen, 6, 161
Strogatz, Steven, 55

Structural holes, 49, 114
Structures
    creation, 34
    interaction, 61–62
Success
    communication/collaboration
        dependence, 119
    prediction, 116–117
Super chickens/flock, 115
Surowiecki, James, 113
Survival of the Friendliest (Hare/
    Woods), 87–88
System
    defining, 19
    expectations, 67
    measurement, 70–72
    operation, determination, 20

T
Tacit knowledge, transfer, 54
Tajfel, Henri, 85
Tall structures, 29–30
    flat structures, contrast, 29f
Tall vertical systems, impact, 29
Task crafting, 95
Task-relevant information, exchange/
    discussion/integration, 113
Teambuilding, usage, 13
Teaming, 115, 153, 165
    agreement, 109–110, 119, 173–178
    business outcome component, 21, 111
    teams, contrast, 112–113
Team of Teams (McChrystal), 28
Teams
    cohesion, 85, 144
    collaboration, encouragement, 26
    creativity/success, 144
    crosscut, addition, 56f
    cross-functional networks, 62
    discomfort, 26
    effectiveness, 5
    empowerment, 110, 153
    goals, attainment (acceleration), 50
    loyal teammates, love, 15

members, 127, 146
norms, 174–175
perfect team, building, 116
performance, enhancement, 50
team-building exercise, 20
teaming, contrast, 112–113
working ability, diagnosis, 175
working norms, informing, 174
Teamwork
EY People Advisory Services
estimates, 112
focus, 67
Temporary work groups
intervention technique, 63
usage, 146
Thinking in Systems (Meadows), 19
Tipping Point, The (Gladwell), 45
Tirole, Jean, 101
Top-down approach, 146–147
Top-down decision-making, 172, 173
Top-level executives, hierarchy
(importance), 25
Top-line revenue targets, sharing, 73
Total Rewards leader, role description, 77
Townsend, Robert, 78
Transaction-based environment, 16
Transformation, realization, 136–137
Tribal behavior, increase, 87
Trust, 146 158, 160–161
cementing force, 42–43
destruction, 27
increase, 17, 88
tracking, 59
Trustworthiness (development), social
relations (usage), 49–50
Turf guarding, absence, 118–119
Tversky, Amos, 103

U
Unbalanced information, 46
Unbalanced network, balanced network
(contrast), 46f
Uncertainty, increase, 31

Up the Organization (Townsend), 78
Upward delegation, avoidance, 136
Us-*versus*-them mentality, 10, 15, 153
Utility, 121, 123–125
characteristics, 124f
purpose/architecture, interrela-
tionship, 122f
Uzzi, Brian, 52

V
Value (values), 132–134
achievement, optimal model, 126–127
addition, structure layer (impact), 33
decisions, alignment, 107
delivery, 25
hierarchy, arrangement, 130f
source, 126
Value-adding process, authority/
accountability (identification), 33
Vertical authority networks, 61
Vertical leverage, concept, 34
Vertical navigation, usage, 30
Vertical structure, 34
Virtual collaboration, 160–164
Virtual work, 158–160
Visual cues, impact (absence), 162

W
Watts, Duncan, 55
Wells Fargo, cross-selling strategy
(absence), 66
Wisdom of Crowds, The (Surowiecki), 113
Work
design, 150
environment, problems, 9
natural flow, disintegration, 33
practices (implementation), employees
(interaction), 34
redesign, 144
responsibility, 165
social features, initiative changes, 95–96
toxic arrangement, 27
Work Disrupted (Schwartz), 163

Workflow
  networks, 61
  reciprocal networks, 61
  reciprocal relationships, team entry, 35
Workforce, experience, 3
Working, boundary spanning, 71
Workplace, 165–167
  burnout, 7

motivation, 14
perception, 16
Wrzesniewski, Amy,
  96

Z
Zanini, Michele, 7
Zoom, usage, 53